Jim Guthrie

WHO NEEDS WHAT

Jim Guthrie

WHO NEEDS WHAT

ANDREW HOOD

Invisible Publishing
Halifax & Toronto

Library and Archives Canada Cataloguing in Publication

Hood, Andrew, 1983-, author
    Jim Guthrie : Who Needs What / Andrew Hood.

(Bibliophonic ; 5)
ISBN 978-1-926743-53-0 (pbk.)

1. Guthrie, Jim. 2. Composers--Canada--Biography.
3. Rock musicians--Canada--Biography. I. Title. II. Series:
Bibliophonic ; 5

ML410.G984H77 2015   782.42166092   C2015-901243-0

Cover by Superbrothers Audiovisual Inc.
Typeset in Laurentian & Slate by Megan Fildes
With thanks to type designer Rod McDonald

Printed and bound in Canada

Invisible Publishing
Halifax & Toronto
www.invisiblepublishing.com

We acknowledge the support of the Canada Council for the Arts which last year invested $20.1 million in writing and publishing throughout Canada.

Invisible Publishing recognizes the support of the Province of Nova Scotia through the Department of Communities, Culture & Heritage. We are pleased to work in partnership with the Culture Division to develop and promote our cultural resources for all Nova Scotians.

Canada Council
for the Arts

Conseil des Arts
du Canada

"Is there any way you can write me in as a supporting character in my own biography?"

— Jim Guthrie

INTRODUCTION

Some Things You Should Know About Sound and Hearing

"The Greek prefix *schizo* means split, separated; and *phone* is Greek for voice. *Schizophonia* refers to the split between an original sound and its electroacoustical transmission and reproduction... Originally all sounds were originals. They occurred at one time in one place only. Sounds were tied to the mechanisms that produced them. The human voice traveled only as far as one could shout. Every sound was uncounterfeitable, unique... Since the invention of electroacoustical equipment for the transmission and storage of sound, any sound, no matter how tiny, can be blown up and shot around the world, or packaged on tape or record for the generations of the future. We have split the sound from the maker of the sound. Sounds have been torn from their natural sockets and given an amplified and independent existence. Vocal sound, for instance, is no longer tied to a hole in the head but is free to issue from anywhere in the landscape."

R. Murray Schafer, *The Tuning of the World* (1997)

In a time of such heavy self-documentation I don't know if this happens much anymore, but there was a while there where you'd hear a recording of your own voice—in the form of a phone message you'd left, say—and insist it wasn't yours. Or you'd at least claim that it didn't *sound* like you, wasn't how you sounded in your head.

What's up is we hear ourselves twofold: from without and from within. We flap our gums and agitate the molecules around us, which enter our ear and drum on our tympanic membrane, bothering our hammer, anvil, and stirrup, which then vibrate some liquid we've got in there, and after that it's all cells and nerve endings and mystery. In this way we hear our own voice from the outside like we'd hear anything else, and we often sound whinier than we think of ourselves sounding. Add to that outward whine our vocal chords humming up through our jawbones—which hitch to our skulls just below the ear—and we get a deeper version of ourselves in our own heads that, if others heard it, might not sound like us to them.

I scooped this bit of sonic trivia from R. Murray Schafer's *The Tuning of the World*, a study of soundscapes I took out of the Guelph Public Library about 10 years ago. It turns out a young Jim Guthrie had been working from the same Schafer text—I assume from the same library copy—almost 20 years before. The quote that introduces this introduction comes from that book, and is also quoted in the liner notes of Jim's 1998 tape *Some Things You Should Know About Sound and Hearing*. A line from *that* quote appears, tinkered with, in the song "Repression's Waltz," on '97's *Documenting Perks Part 1*. It goes: "Back in a time when my voice only travelled

2

as far as I could shout, I delivered my sermon of doubt."

I was drunk for the first time the summer of 2001. This was also, coincidentally, the first time I tried hitting on a girl. I made my move—as a best I could—by vicing a set of head-phones on her, plugged into a Discman with *A Thousand Songs*[1] poised on track 23, and insisting she listen to "Repression's Waltz."

I was in England doing a high school creative writing credit. The kids I was abroad with were mostly from in and around Toronto, were mostly well-to-do, were mostly more experienced than I was. That night I'd been hauled out to some club and took a liking to this drink called Vodka Blue, which tasted enough like blue popsicles that I didn't mind drinking a lot of it. Newly in my cups, I found I didn't com-pletely hate myself for the first time in a long time, and so insisted this girl I'd taken a Blue shine to listen to something I thought was important and rare.

As dwarfed as I felt by these well-travelled kids, I learned pretty quickly that I was into and down with all this stuff that was news to them. I was ripping off Kurt Vonnegut and quot-ing *Kids in the Hall*, and in my 12-disc carrying case I had the first four albums from Three Gut Records: *A Thousand Songs*, Royal City's *At Rush Hour the Cars*, Gentleman Reg's *The Theoretical Girl*, and the first Constantines album. Never mind that I'd never been on a subway, been drunk, or kissed anybody. There in London, sitting on the curb while these Toronto kids smoked a little ways off, I felt like I was a part

---

[1] *A Thousand Songs* is a ménage of Jim's early tapes and new material.

of something very special, and—lips stained a bit blue—felt like that made me special.

So I had this girl listen to "Repression's Waltz," and stared boozy-eyed at her while she did. She put her hands on the headphones like they might fly off and looked at me looking at her, smiling and nodding to confirm that she was hearing something.

There're at least three guitars in "Waltz," playing mostly minor chords at first, one in your right ear, one in your left, one in the middle of your hearing. Each guitar is sluggish, a bit doleful, struggling to catch up with the other and play the same song. You can hear the chair Jim was sitting on creak throughout and he sounds pooped and sings with marbles in his mouth. The right, left, and centre Jims finally find one another as the song crescendos into major chords, and Jim sings, "Give in to your undying love for me."

I'd forgotten about that part.

While all the Jims were urging a massive concession to love, the girl handed back my headphones and smiled politely. "Neat," she said. "Sad. Kinda weird." She was nice about it and left to get a cigarette from somebody.

Though special to me, this is not a special story. And no doubt it's boring on account of its ubiquity. But let's not undervalue the bigness of shared experience. Every kid who came up in a time of accessible and sharable media has probably forced someone they were excited about to listen to a song or watch a video or read a book they similarly had a boner for.

The act of sharing this stuff is an attempt at shorthand, especially at ages when we haven't really figured out exactly who and how we are. The message to people we're trying to impress or smooch is as much "This is what I like" as it is "This is what I *am* like."

A Thousand Songs was the perfect thing at the perfect time for me. Who knows what kind of bumbling, vicious meathead I would have turned into if not for that album. The day of Jim's Guelph release of *A Thousand Songs*, I'd gone to see the matinee of *American Pie*. In the summer of '99 I was making a transition between the dude buddies I'd had since elementary school and these new hippy-ish girls I'd met in high school. The former whipped batteries at each other during lunch in the tech hall; the latter made their own pants and were vegetarians. I caught the Pie Fucking Movie with the one gang and, that night, went to the CD release—*in a bar*—with the other. Jim wasn't exactly a left fielder. I was then dipping a toe into Ween and They Might Be Giants. Both bands seemed to love pop as much as they hated it, made fun of what they did as much as they took it seriously. They sounded like nothing else and like absolutely everything.

I just went to the show to go. I didn't know that this Jim Guthrie guy was a Guelph celebrity who had granted, fostered, and participated in a far-reaching permission to make and disseminate music in my hometown, whose cassettes full of tape-hissy, half-song/half-sound experiments were coveted by these patchouli-smelling peers I was making inroads with, one of whom had named her goldfish Jim Guthrie. For all its importance, two things most stand out about that show[2]. First, I remember the lead singer of By

---

2 August 7ish, 1999. Jim would do a dual launch in Toronto with Leslie Feist and her first album, *Monarch (Lay Your Jeweled Head Down)* at the Rivoli on August 24.

Divine Right, José Contreras, was there. BDR's "Come For A Ride" video was all over MuchMusic at the time, so I figured this guy was rich and famous, and didn't understand why he'd be in Guelph for this dingy bar show. Second, everyone was sitting down cross-legged, and, for this entire show that would go on to change my life a bit, I was mostly worrying that my ass crack was winking at the people behind me.

A Thousand Songs sounds and smells like that transitional summer to me, feels like those new people I was meeting, the person I was becoming. Two years later, when I left Guelph for university I would walk around Montreal listening to that album and cry a bit whenever the organ came whining in on "Roads and Paper Routes[3]," describing my homesickness better than I could at the time.

You came to see Jim Guthrie and instead are being forced to look at the ass crack of the chubby redhead sitting cross-legged in front of you. But this is important: this is both a declaration of bias and an introduction to the fact that this book about Jim Guthrie is not always about Jim Guthrie.

Since 1989, Jim's been making music alone or with a few buds in one basement or another, except for a while in the 2000s when he was in a pantry. For someone so independent Jim's been a vital member, contributor, and progenitor of a handful of communities and scenes across his more than 20 active years of making music. From a small-town DIY rock movement in the mid-90s, to a post-millennium indie Renaissance that laid a lot of ground work for today's national

---

3 See: 3:52 minutes in.

music scene, to a jangly angle that would define a new wave of ad music, and most recently, to innovations in video game scoring that exposed Jim to a devout global audience. But, like some rock and roll Mennonite, Jim has been in these worlds, but not always of them.

"He was very much an island to himself," is how composer Owen Pallett puts it. "He was the guy making the best records and taking the most chances, but he also had the sparest of career ambitions, no apparent desire to be a touring musician."

Beyond the quality and consistency of the work itself, Jim's success is often thanks to his compatibility with other artists and go-getters; people who saw a bit of themselves in what Jim was doing, people who Jim maybe saw a bit of himself in. These people, from different places and for different reasons, have been putting Jimful headphones on as many kids as they can, saying, "Have you *heard* this?"

This is often a book about those people as much as it is about Jim[4].

I'm willing to chalk that up to schizophonia. With the sound split from its maker, it becomes peripatetic. Wandering, the music finds us, the listener. When we take it in, include it in our life and the things we do, it becomes stuck to a whole new place. We become the new source, "the mechanism," as Schaffer puts it. Our experience with the music returns it to a sort of state of uncounterfeitability,

---

4 Mind you, there are more people left out of this book than included in it—many of whom gifted me their time and memories and opinions. If your voices aren't directly here, they're certainly holding much of this book up. I'm sorry and thank you.

of uniqueness. It's as though the sound without matches up with something more elusive and fundamental within, giving that trebly outer sound an inner richness. Music goes from being the voice we hear on an answering machine—the voice that everyone hears the same—to the voice we hear in our own heads. This stuff that doesn't have anything to do with us starts to sound so specifically like us.

CHAPTER 1

How We Get Old

"Where's Jim?"
"Outside being useless."
– from *River's Edge*
(as quoted in "River's Edge" from *Victim of Lo-Fi*)

When I bug Aaron Riches for his memories of the young James Edward Guthrie he met at Waverley Drive PS, he laughs: "Jim had the exact same haircut as he does now. He really looked the same. Jim hasn't changed. I think he was born how he is.

"Of course..." Aaron tempers his amusement some. "Everyone grows."

Three quarters of what would become Royal City met at this time, at Waverley. Both Aaron and Jim are Guelph-born. Simon Osborne, bassist for that band and player on most of Jim's albums, moved from Ottawa in Grade 7.

Simon was into skateboarding and made friends that way after relocating. Through a skating friend he heard about this "cool guy from across the street" who had a Vision Psycho

Stick[5] and could do kickflips. "So I met Jim," he remembers, "and he could do the kickflips that were described. And I thought Jim seemed pretty awesome, too."

The earliest first Jimpression comes from Steve McCuen, childhood chum and collaborator on a hard-to-place project, Mandrills[6]. In "Rap Song 2000," Steve rhymes his memories of first meeting Jim: "I can remember being back in grade 3 / It's in September—'82—it's where I first met Guthrie... He sold his Mite-Y-Mite bike to my younger brother Mike / and told us how to ghost ride the damn bike."

"I just remember getting huge laughs," Jim recalls when I ask him about ghost riding, a trick where you leave a moving bike and it continues independent of you. "You did that and everyone'd be on the grass. If you could make a bunch of kids laugh by having skill enough to jump off your bike in such a way that it coasts silently... I was one of those kids who had, like, no confidence, but who had hand-eye coordination.

"And I could throw a rock," he goes on, "Like, really far. Or straight up in the air and everyone would be like, 'Holy shit!' You couldn't even see it anymore. And it would take 30 seconds to hit the ground. I remember moments like that. Just doing little things that gained immediate [attention].

"Even still... I went to the cottage with a few people [recently] and I pulled out the ol' rock throwin' arm, and I still had it. I always attributed it to a good, stout frame. And I have

---

5 A neon, condom-shaped skateboard deck that was apparently coveted then.
6 Mandrills is mostly off-the-cuff recordings made since 2000-ish anytime Jim visits Steve in Montreal. Songs were available on Jim's website for a time, and I'm sure a bit of patient Googling will yield something or other. The band's bio runs: "Jim is a music genius, Steve's a lil weird."

these whippy, elasticy arms. I think there's a real kind of physics there. I think if you got somebody to measure my body, they'd be like, 'This is optimal. These are the dimensions you'd use to build one of those David and Goliath slingshots.'

"I made one of those [slingshots], too. When I was younger I used to be really crafty and self-reliant. But the whole while I was trying to choke down a stutter."

Two years older than Jim, Stephen Evans met Jim on the block. "He was about 12 or 13," he says. "I think I remember him stammering a lot and being quite shy, but he was also very athletic. He was built like a little gymnast. He was an amazing skateboarder and he was an amazing breakdancer. Well, not an amazing breakdancer, but he spent time learning that stuff. He could moonwalk. I didn't know anybody who could moonwalk.

"He moves so beautifully, this little man."

But Stephen stresses that Jim was never a show-off. "I think he just liked devoting himself to learning something and seeing if he could pull it off."

Jim's character, like his music, is a unique balance of reservation and razzmatazz. He's never been someone to trumpet a project, but the work itself, and his dedication to it, has always had such a visible aplomb that drawing attention is inevitable.

To hear it from Jim's friends, the guy stood out in adolescence; to hear it from Jim, it was the opposite. "When I was younger," he says, "I didn't like being the centre of attention because normally, when I was the centre of attention, I was stuttering in front of a class. So I sort of learned being the centre of attention doesn't always feel good.

"I used to think of myself as a bit of a Seabiscuit[7]," he says. "In as much as Seabiscuit is sort of a lame horse that nobody wanted. I wasn't super book smart when I was younger, and I had that stutter, and when I was born my legs were all kinda twisted and turned in. I had to wear casts on my legs for the first little bit of my life. I was always just sorta short and runty. Now that's all in the past, and I guess it was a big deal at the time. Now, when I put [those issues] under a microscope, they all seem like big little things, a great deal of who I was when I was younger.

"But I learned a lot from those early struggles and it sort of showed me how to adapt and reinvent myself over the years."

Split grades separated Jim and Steve McCuen for most of elementary school, but they met up again in junior high. They were still into *MAD* magazine, but by the eighth grade were also getting into *The Watchmen* and Frank Miller's revamping of the DC Comics mainstays. The tone of *MAD* and the grittiness of this new wave in the mainstream made for an easy transition to underground comics. If they could find him, they were reading Crumb.

It was a confluence of the comics and hip hop that helped them shake their early musical interests—for Jim, Howard Jones; for Steve, Phil Collins. "By '89, De La Soul had dropped *Three Feet High and Rising*," Steve says. "We were hip hop. We loved it. But then by '91, Sonic Youth was sing-

---

7 The tiny, unlikely racehorse that became a winner and testament to the rewards of perseverance to a Depression-era U.S.

ing with Public Enemy[8], and we were like, 'Sonic Youth might be cool.' When [hip hop] started getting all dolla dolla bills and bitches and hos, we sort of said, 'Okay, let's differentiate ourselves from this misogyny and become *alternative.*'"

While the coming 'alternative' influences of bands like Sebadoh, Pavement, Ween, They Might Be Giants, and, later, The Sea and Cake, and Tortoise, would shape much of Jim's work throughout the 90s, Jim's post-millennium love of licks and movement towards a more polished production is anchored by a parallel influence of classic rock. "Jim was into Queen before it was cool," Steve explains. "Where I turned to, say, Elvis Costello because of his big words, Jim was into Queen for the production. He was all, 'Let's smoke some hash and listen to this with headphones.'"

The metal influences came from his older sister Jenn and her boyfriend. "Rick was this heavy metal guitarist dude straight out of *Dazed and Confused*," Stephen Evans remembers. "I know that Jim spent tons of time learning to play guitar from Rick. Metal music and classic rock leading up to metal, Led Zeppelin kind of stuff."

But when we're talking exposure, Stephen himself was a sort of patient zero. "[He] was the guy who was a little bit older, who was going to college, who knew all the cool bands way before we all did," Jim says. "He came home with the single of 'Smells Like Teen Spirit' months before it broke. I remember jumping up and down on the bed with a beer in my hand for three hours thinking 'This is the best fucking

---

8 Sonic Youth opened for Public Enemy on December 29, 1990, at the Aragon Ballroom in Chicago

song.' Stephen was Mr. College Radio. I didn't go to college, so he was my link to a lot of cool new music."

"I used to be a real music hound," Stephen says. "I'd really sleuth out music in magazines and on college radio. And then I'd come back for visits and show my friends all the stuff I'd collected and learned."

It bears stressing the obvious, that this was ante-internet. Zines, college radio, word-of-mouth, and past-your-bedtime TV shows were your best bets for finding new music. If you found a new band, you'd figure out what label they were on and try to wrangle more of that catalogue, or you'd try to identify who was playing and find other bands they were in, who the other members of these farflung regional scenes were. Or you'd read *Sassy* magazine, which is where Jim and Stephen found out about Ween, featured once in *Sassy's* "Cute Band Alert[9]."

"I think we bought a few issues," Stephen confesses. "Because we were interested in girls and we wanted to know these kinds of details." Instead, it led to all of them "getting into Ween and smoking pot."

"Ultimately," Steve McCuen says, "what you'd want to know is the summer of '89, when Jimmy's 16, he gets an acoustic guitar."

"It was actually a log of an acoustic guitar that hurt to play," Jim specifies. "It had no business being called a guitar." Later, Jim bought an electric off the same guy. A Japanese Telecaster for $175. "A total steal and it felt like

---

9 April '92. The cover features the then-it couple Kurt Cobain and Courtney Love.

heaven in my hands. It looked exactly like the one Ralph Macchio used to 'cut heads' in *Crossroads*."

Though a late-bloomer by some standards, Jim had early on showed an un-fostered knack for music.

"I was always able to hear and understand music," he says, "but I wasn't really aware that I had the sort of right to take action on what I understood, you know, in my head. I'm not overly gifted. I'm not overly Beethoven.

"I remember being at a friend's house and he had a piano, and I never had pianos growing up, and I was maybe seven or eight. We're watching TV, and I was sitting [at the piano] and an ad comes on. I sort of hear it, and there's four notes, and I find those notes. I fumble a couple of times, but I just play it back and he turns to me and says, 'How did you do that?' And I wasn't able to really articulate it. But in my mind I was sort of thinking, 'Don't you hear that?'

"I guess figuring out that jingle was one of the first times I realized I could hear something. Not that it was super-special, but it was my first own realization."

With the same dedication he'd given to breakdancing and skateboarding and ghost riding, Jim took on the guitar, and anything else he could get a sound out of.

"I think this is just as I was getting to know him [again],'" says Simon Osborne. "He started diversifying. You know, there are guys who are like, 'I have my acoustic guitar and that's it.' But Jim would buy some weird little drum, or find a keyboard in a thrift shop and bring it home."

Since junior high, Simon had veered away from Jim and Steve McCuen, concentrating more on skateboarding. "When I quit [skating]," he says, "I just wanted a clean break, so I made this shift of friends. Gradually I got brought into the 'Jim circle,' which was, I don't know, sort of 'the artsy burn out gang.'"

"Apparently at John F. Ross [high school], some people thought that we were acid heads and dropped acid all the time," confirms Beate Schwirtlich, who went to a different high school[10], but met Jim and Steve McCuen around grade 11. Answering to the veracity of those acid rumours, she laughs, "Somewhat, yeah. Some of the time."

The meat of their Arty Burnout time was spent yakking and goofing in Arby's. "Those guys would spend hours there," says Beate. "And it was all about drinking as much coffee as possible. They had free refills. I don't know if other teenagers just hung out and talked that much. All those guys are really funny, and humour is really creative. Whether they were failing every subject [in school] or not, you could tell they were smart guys. Real people who are intelligent and nice is what I was drawn to. And they didn't take themselves too seriously, which I liked."

The other prime spot for gathering was Jim's room, filled with art and Queen posters and an accumulation of gear and instruments. "That basement constantly smelled like cat piss," Stephen Evans says. "We would always hang out there, because we could smoke."

Just as Jim was hitting a musical stride, high school ended and he was expected to carry on to college. His parents figured an art degree.

---

10 Guelph Collegiate and Vocational Institute, where Aaron Riches was then a strong presence and organizer of a hardcore punk scene most notable for bringing Fugazi to Guelph, their first Canadian date.

"Before I got into music," he told artist Dan Berry[11] on the podcast Make It Then Tell Everybody, "I was pretty convinced I was gonna do some form of visual arts. I would draw comics, Steve McCuen would draw comics, and we sort of taught each other as we were growing up."

To satisfy his parents, Jim applied to Sheridan College; to satisfy himself, he flubbed the application. "One thing you had to do," he says, "was draw your own hand and so I drew my own hand with my wrong hand. And I just handed in a really pathetic [application]... Nothing I was proud of. I knew that what I wanted out of life wasn't at school, but at the time I couldn't have told you what that was exactly."

If we're weighing influence, maybe Steve McCuen kicked Jim's ass hardest. "He was the first one," Jim explains, "when we were 16 or 17, to just say, 'I'm an artist.' My first response was, 'No you're not. You're just a guy.' But he sorta taught me that life and art and being who you are is really personal. You don't need a degree and all that. It sort of seems obvious now, but it was a big deal to me back then. If I can just call myself an artist, why do I need to go to school?"

Jim went to McDonald's instead, doing overnight maintenance: draining fryers, cleaning the sundae machines, mopping. "That was one good thing about my parents," he says. "[When I didn't get into school], they were like 'Well, you're not just sitting in the basement.'"

Jim's shift ran midnight til eight. "I remember when he worked [there]," says Beate. "He got so he could get his cleaning done really early and he would take his amp and

---

11 Dan did the video of *Takes Time*'s "The Rest Is Yet To Come"

play guitar in the middle of the night."

The banging pots and pans that opens "I Don't Wanna Be A Rock Star" were recorded in that McDonald's lobby, performed on upturned condiment trays. "I just turned it into this crazy noise-fest thing," Jim recalls, "and started screaming."

"He probably wasn't a very good employee," Beate laughs.

Being from Guelph, I'm making the very Guelph-like mistake of assuming everyone knows where/what Guelph is. Driving West along Highway 401, it'll cost you about an hour to get from Toronto to Guelph, as well-known for its university and veterinary college as it is for all the rock that came and still comes out of it. John McCrea and Robert Munsch are from Guelph, and so is actress Neve Campbell[12].

Guelph's downtown core is a sometimes uncomfortable mix of blue collar pool players and obliterated first year students. In Montreal I was in a creative writing workshop with Spencer Krug, who passed through Guelph to play a show with Wolf Parade one weekend[13]. At next week's workshop, Spencer described coming down into the street after the show and being passed by a running, howling kid covered in blood, some dude wielding a wine bottle in pursuit. That sounded about right.

But by dint of its university town-ness, Guelph has always had and still has a stalwart, sometimes renowned art and

---

12 Much of the original Royal City press at some point included a story about how Neve Campbell once smooched Aaron Riches.
13 Friday September 12th 2003 at Ed Video, with Arcade Fire, Barmitzvah Brothers, and Cryin' Out Loud Choir

music scene. For 30 years it's been home to the Hillside Festival, and a jazz festival for about 20. Aboveground, a few of the Rheostatics records were released by the label DROG[14], and, in the early 90s, bands like Black Cabbage and King Cobb Steelie were Guelph-based. Underground, there's never been any shortage of kids getting up to something.

Nick Craine, member of Black Cabbage, hosted an open stage on Sunday nights at a pop-up venue, the Mercury Café, in the early 90s. "You'd get these [same] two hippies who would always come up and do the same three songs," he says. "And there was one sax player who was technically very good, but a real dick. And then who should come upon it one day but a young Jim Guthrie[15]."

Jim hadn't told any of his friends he was playing. It wasn't out of any kind of ambition beyond challenging himself that Jim took a stab at playing live. "I got to a certain age," he says, "where I understood that if you have fears, it's maybe good to face them head on. So it was a huge deal for me to get on stage the first time."

Jim's position in the sign-up sheet approached and, antsy with memories of unwanted attention while stuttering, he went to Nick for advice:

"'Nick,'" I said, 'I'm so nervous right now, I'm gonna die.'

---

14 Dave's Records of Guelph, run by Cowboy Junkies Dave Teichroeb and Lewis Melville.

15 Jim doesn't recall exactly when this was, and neither does Nick. "It could have been '92," he says. "It gets blurry." There's a fog drifting through this book as though it were a Hammer Horror. Post-millennium machinations show up on public record, but before then, most facts rely on the memories of the interviewees, every one of which apologized for the haze of memory.

"And [Nick] said, 'You know, if you can relax enough to take a shit before you play, that usually helps.'

"Like, he leaned over and said it like this great... I mean, it *was* great advice. But not nearly as profound [as I thought it would be]. Also very profound in a way. But I did, I tried. I went to the bathroom to be relaxed. Because, you know, you have to be a certain amount of relaxed to play."

"And then he came out and played this stuff," remembers Nick. "It was like math-rock. It was like Southern Ontario Phillip Glass music. Really textural, really interesting.

"Jim's delivery comes from a meek place, from a place that's humble. It comes from a place that's not well represented. It asks your permission to be there. Most music barges into the room and says, 'Look at me!' But Jim's voice clearly says, 'I'd like to have your permission to share this with you. That's the impression I got [that night]. That's why people recognize it instantly. [The music] says '*We're* the protagonist, not *me.*'

"And I think after that [the owner] gave him his own slot opening up for Aaron Riches[16]."

"'Opening up for,'" Aaron confirms, laughing dismissively at how earnest that sounds.

---

16 Aaron at that point had moved away from hardcore punk to more troubadour-y folk, putting out two albums on DROG, the second of which, *Rain*, was produced by Nick Craine. Leslie Feist's first music video, "It's Cool to Love Your Family," was directed by Nick as well and featured all the members of Royal City.

CHAPTER 2

The Royal City Home Rock Eruption

"If I only could / I'd take a bite out of this town /
spit up / and pass it around." – "Repression's Waltz"

Unbeknownst to me at the time, downtown Guelph was a
fecund place to be in the 90s, busy with as many rock shows
then as it is with fistfights and ticketings for public urination
now. Weiner that I was, I'd mostly venture down to get my hair
cut at a salon in the shopping centre or exchange some single-
based CanRock CD I'd got from Columbia House at whatever
long-since-closed record store. The high school hardcore
scene of the late-80s and early-90s had kept on keeping on
but as the explosion of Nirvana and this new "alternative"
music lent light to less-explored tunnels and tributaries of the
underground, the lone farting-around of individuals like Jim
was brought into a new, more organisable context.

"When I first bought a 4-track and started playing shows
('92 – '93)," Jim wrote to *Wavelength*, a weekly showcase
that served as a launching pad for some of the best music

to come out of Toronto since 2000, "the underground local music scene [in Guelph] was incredible. Everybody was making music and everybody had their own sound. It was weird because at any given show you would hear some of the craziest rock you'd ever heard and nobody was self-conscious, everyone was really into what they were doing. It was a lot of hard work but nobody cared because we all felt like we were sharing something more important."

"It was kind of a resurgent hippie generation," admits Stewart Gunn, member of that scene and half, along with Colin Clark, of the Sonic Bunny cassette label. "Everybody was just trying to love everybody else.

"There was a really wide range of music being made, and a lot of good music. A lot of people got involved because they had the support to get involved. So there were lots of people making music who had no long-term musical ambition or no particular musical skill. And in the centre of that was a guy like Jim, who was obviously a skilled musician who had honed his craft and was continuing to do so. But he would have been doing whatever whenever; you got the sense that he was driven by something more than the convenience of it."

A CD released as a fundraiser for CFRU, the University of Guelph radio station, *The Goods: A Guelph Compilation* amounts to something of a class photo of that scene. Genre-wise, you've got your folk, traditional, post-rock, pop, hip hop, punk, spoken word, and whatever heartbreaking plinking you want to call Jim's "How we get old." It gives you a good sense of how varied such a small scene was. But when you take a look at the personnel, do a head count, the players don't vary as much as the sound.

If you're a collector of Canadian indie rock, *The Goods* is full of rookie cards. You find Aaron Riches here, Tim Kingsbury, Jamie Thompson, Reg "Gentleman Reg" Vermue, Liz Powell, Noah 23, Evan Gordon, and Megali Meagher. As members of and contributors to the likes of Arcade Fire, the Unicorns, Islands, Land of Talk, the Hidden Cameras, and Broken Social Scene, these are kids who would go on to help articulate a sound and an energy that repopulated the sere fallout left by—amongst other factors—major label mishandling of an earlier generation of artists.

"I think we were all naturally sceptical of that sort of ambition [to be successful]," says Tim Kingsbury, now of Arcade Fire, of Gentleman Reg and the Stealth Cats and the Stewart Gunn Band then. "It was really more about having fun and looking for interesting things without an end in mind."

But if we're calling *The Goods* a class photo, let's specify: it's a graduation sitting. These shaggy-haired, grinning kids mostly had one foot out of town. And what was special about Guelph's output, that tangible verve and perspicacity that you can find laced into so much of what's happening in Canadian music now, was already stressing the seams of the place itself.

Properly exploring the parentage of this scene would turn into the worst kind of Maury Pauvich episode. Everybody was influencing everybody in that hot tub of 90s Guelph—"A super soup of influence," as Jim calls it. But to source the spirit of the scene, we can microscope the idea of "home rock," a phrase and an ideology that animated these pockets of Guelph.

Addressing a lack of women programmers, CFRU put out a call for new hosts in '91. Still in high school, Beate Schwirtlich got herself a slot. The Screaming Virgins Radio Show aired Friday nights from 12 – 2 a.m. Beate had been to the station plenty for parties or rock shows before seeing the ad. "CFRU at the time, honestly, you went there and partied," she says. "You smoked and brought booze. If you had a late-night show, there might be a scene going on."

"It was a great place to hang out," Stephen Evans agrees. "Goof around, get drunk, get high, discover music together."

The 10 p.m. show leading into Beate's, Rock Show, was hosted by Gord High. A few years older than Beate, Gord was a Fine Arts student. "He had a genius IQ," she says, "and had a way of believing in people and would motivate you to have confidence to do [things] and to want to do it, and make it seem fun. We started having these Tuesday night rock nights. I didn't know how to play guitar, so I learned jamming with him."

Gord recorded these sessions on his 4-track. A home version of a studio multi-track, the 4-track made it possible to record, as the name implies, four different tracks onto one cassette.

It was through Beate that Jim met Gord. "He was totally different than anyone I knew," he remembers. "You almost feared Gord. He was this grumpy guy who smoked a lot of cigarettes, but was super intelligent and played guitar like nobody I knew. He taught me how to do-it-for-yourself, and how a lot of other people who are famous did it for themselves, how every scene started from nothing."

"In his apartment," Beate remembers, "he had this stupid

poster that said HOME BAKING. He got it from a thrift store and it was meant to be in a restaurant, with pictures of pies or something like that on it. The idea was store-bought versus homemade. Home baking, home fries, home *rock*. His thing with home rock was to motivate people to just do it yourself, and do it cheap."

"Gord was one of the first people who truly hit home [to me] how little of a plan you needed to make music," says Jim, "how little you needed. There's just something about the creative process where you have to throw yourself into it. You just turn up the amps and go. I was maybe a little bit more careful with my own ideas. Whereas Gord was more like, 'Don't even talk about what you're playing, just start.' He was way more experimental, and taught me how to go with an idea with no real idea of where it's going.

"It was really hard to figure out what would please Gord, but the whole time [he] was only asking you to be you[17]. That's a big part of understanding the whole Home Is Where The Rock Is philosophy: just stay home and be yourself. Don't chase the rock, let it come to you. I could split hairs, but let's just say I didn't know anything [before] I met Gord. I had my own little sliver of indie rock figured out," Jim explains, "but he turned me on to so many things musically, technically, and philosophically.

"One day, up at CFRU, Gord was going on a tangent about how you should just stay home and make music. 'Why do

---

17 Gord passed away after a lengthy battle with leukemia in January 2012. He was 40. A bench dedicated to Gord reads: "HOME ROCK" BECAUSE HOME IS WHERE THE ROCK IS.

you need to go out and buy things? Just stay home and play guitar.' And I was like, 'Well Gord, you know why? Because home is where the heart is.'

"And he was like, 'No, Jim. Home is where the *rock* is.' He totally blew my mind. I think it's safe to say that Gord is the Godfather of the Guelph Home Rock scene and I was one of his children."

"It wasn't long before everyone owned a 4-track," Jim told *Wavelength*, "and a tidal wave of home rock left us waxing up our surfboards. In an attempt to preserve all that was happening I hosted a radio show up at the University of Guelph."

A jewellers case for this scattered output, The Royal City Home Rock Eruption[18] aired on CFRU, Wednesdays from 3 to 4 p.m. Jim either already had the tapes, or they were sent to the station, or stuffed into his mailbox. He put up anything these kids were laying down.

"I sounded like a total turd," Jim admits. "I had nothing intelligent to say, but I guess that wasn't the point. If you were 14 I might've sounded like I knew what I was talking about, but I was struggling."

Lucky for Jim, plenty listeners were in that age range. Local lore has high school kids tuning in at the back of the class, putting a varnish on Jim's influence and importance in the eyes of a younger crowd.

"I was nervous," he says, "but it was another one of my self-therapy tactics. It was like I was working on my fear of

---

18 A nod to both the John Spencer Blues Explosion and Lou Barlow's Folk Implosion.

public speaking but I was alone in the room so it was cool. But mostly it was fun and important to me, not to mention the group of people who listened every week. Never making a note, never having recorded anything in your life and then having someone play it on a radio station… [It] got people to come out of their shells."

"There was always cool stuff," remembers Tim Kingsbury. "People would send him stuff that they'd just cooked up. It was pretty great. Now you can just post stuff to a message board, but at the time you had to tune in to listen to home-made stuff."

With acts and artists like Sebadoh, Pavement, and Ween increasingly visible, these surges of DIY were happening in small-town Petri dishes all over.

Punk's legacy has mostly been reduced, culturally, to a sound and style. And as much as it turned into a recalibration of how music is played and what people look like while they're playing it, whatever punk was and continues to be is essentially an ongoing granting of permission—a constant reminder that what's being done inside a pre-existing system can just as easily be done outside of it. To be a musician, all you have to do is make music. It's a fascicle switch to flip, sure, but finding any switch can be tricky and embarrassing when the room's dark.

The availability of home recording technology, like the affordable, lap-sized 4-track, and a mid-80s surge of experimental and sonically loose rock flipped the switch for less-obviously talented kids, giving them a sort of cheap, idiot-proof way to muck around with music. You could just turn up your amp and go.

Talking about his cornerstone lo-fi submission, *The Freed Man*, Sebadoh's Lou Barlow wrote, "This record was intended to be a mess. A stinking garden of delights." High levels of unencumbered creativity defines lo-fi as much as low levels of sonic clarity. These albums tend to be generic grab bags, albums poured to the meniscus with the sort of vim and risk that rarely survives the demoing stage. They're wildfires compared to controlled burns of studio albums. And while the sound might not always be for everybody, it announces that anybody can do it.

Upon first hearing pre-"Loser" Beck, put out by K Records, Stewart Gunn recalls that shift in understanding: "This guy doesn't have any more than me. He's got a 4-track and a shitty old guitar and this guy is actually making a living doing what I do—granted with a little more fineness. For me, the whole idea of a tape label became viable when I realized that there were people around the world [doing this]. It wasn't just me and Colin [Clark] with our 4-track.

"Jim's radio show, as far as what was happening in Guelph at the time, was sort of the glue that, in many ways, was holding the whole independent music scene together," says Stewart.

"For us it was personal," Colin stresses. "Anybody felt like they could put something on tape and Jim'd play it. And he'd put it up with other great indie rock. He'd play it even if he didn't like it. I think he understood the ethic of what it meant to make something in your bedroom and send it outside. I think he understood, having done it, what it meant to make something and share it."

"I don't know why we even started a tape label," Colin marvels. Both from rural parts of slightly Northern Ontario, Colin Clark and Stewart Gunn met at summer school in Barrie. "Stewart was a punk," says Colin, "and I was just kinda angry." In 1995, at 15, Colin moved to Guelph. Stewart wasn't far behind. The first few tapes in the Sonic Bunny catalogue were just the two of them, together or apart, and leaned towards the more cacophonous, Sonic Youth-y end of the lo-fi spectrum. "We made stickers and stuck them on telephone poles downtown. And then, about two weeks later, we got this bizarre letter [written] in marker—about three different colours of marker: 'Hi. I'm Jim Guthrie. I make indie rock. I have a radio show. I'd like to meet you guys. Maybe you could come on the show.'"

"Yeah," friend Darcie Clark confirms. "He used marker. And he would address his letters to me 'From Poopy Pants.'"

A punk and an angry young man, Stewart and Colin went onto The Eruption as guests and tried to upturn the love-filled apple cart. "We were like, 'Fuck indie rock. We're doing it *real.*'" Jim's response was to gang up with them, in spite of their "awkward attempt at polemics," as Colin calls their guest spot. "He was like, 'I really like the idea of a cassette label in Guelph. Would you like this album that I've already made and shared with people? And you could put it out?'"

"I vaguely remember Stewart and I freaking out, like 'Holy shit! This is the real deal.'"

"To us, [putting out Jim's tape] did mean some sort of legitimacy," says Stewart. Selling tapes at rock shows, Jim's were always the first to go. "Because it meant that we had on our label an artist that people actually wanted to buy. The other music was very, very scattered. There's not a whole lot there that I could go back to without feeling a little embarrassed. But Jim's music was direct, and it had passion, and he was taking it seriously. So it gave us a feeling of actually having a purpose as a label. And, for Jim, I think the fact that Colin and I weren't shy, and we were really in your face, really hyped up on the ignorant passion of youth, I think Jim maybe saw that as a way to balance his own natural reluctance."

Built from recordings made between '92 and '95, *Home Is Where The Rock Is* blends nicely into the copse of its influences, and, to a certain extent, takes a major load off on its lo-fi laurels. But when we're talking first volleys, the tape's listenable as hell. A collection initially made for friends, it's a friendly tape. Like a lot of Jim's more polished work to come, you feel like you're being included in something small and personal, a quality in itself that's an almost subliminal element of lo-fi. These are albums being made in bedrooms, living rooms, basements—domestic, real spaces, as opposed to the manufactured, arguably fictional spaces of a recording studio. The phone rings, cars drive by, cats mewl. You feel like you're over visiting. And while Jim's moved away from what is audibly lo-fi, he's always managed to maintain the homey, home rockiness of it.

"*Home Is Where The Rock Is* is the one I can't listen to," Jim confesses. "That's the one where I hear the identity crisis. Every [tape] after that, I hear the struggle and progress of an individual trying to find themselves and artistically, you know, give voice to what they're wrestling with. But that first one is maybe too earnest. I just hear the innocence, which makes me uncomfortable."

Jim's discomfort aside, that first tape amounts to a sort of Big Bang of his universe. So many of the core elements of his sturdier creations are present here, even if they're nascent and scruffy. There's the guilt-free interest in the hook, in ear worms, that will go on to feed Jim's more pop-oriented "singer-songwriter" sallies as well as his shot to the ad world's arm. If he doesn't quite know how to make a song sound good, the McDonald's employee on that tape knows what a good song sounds like. Most impressive, though, are the sound experiments that weed up out of Jim's AM radio sidewalk. On this first tape, as limited as his means might've been, there are inklings of an interest in what sound and noise can convey that chords and lyrics can't.

"You listen to so much music," says Mark Goldstein, now poet and then drummer for By Divine Right, who would play Jim's tapes constantly in the tour van, "and then you hear something like that, and you're like 'What the fuck is this? This is awesome.' I remember instantly loving Jim's sensibility, his nervousness, his exploratory energies. Hearing Jim, I realized that he was drawing on a world of American avant-garde, especially at a time when people were uptight about that shit, leaning more towards Seattle. For me, Jim felt like an anomaly."

Through the 90s, Jim played live on his own so rarely I wouldn't be surprised if kids made wishes on his solo shows. As a contributor, though, you couldn't huck a rock in Guelph without hitting an act that Jim was in. Of the 15 bands featured on *The Goods*, Jim appears in roughly a quarter. And if Jim wasn't playing in your band, chances are he put you guys to tape[19].

Kids started quitting their own basements, going to Jim's to record. Dubbed The Roksac[20] that place was and remains a dumpy brick house in a Guelph neighbourhood called The Ward, about a 10-minute walk to downtown across the river. "Another real shit hole," in the words of Stephen Evans. I popped by there just after moving day, July 2014. By the side of the road there was a purple and black Legend snowboard and, fittingly, a box of pots and pans that weren't good for anything other than drumming on. Being a guy who doesn't uproot himself that easily, it took being nearly killed in a car accident in October '95 to get Jim out of his parent's basement and into that so-called shit hole.

"He got blown out of his fucking shoes," chuckles Beate, with some remnant disbelief. She was in there with him. "It was in the early days of the SUV rollover. We roll, and everyone who's wearing their seatbelts is still in the car, and there's no Jim. When we found him he wasn't wearing any shoes. They were in the car because they weren't done up properly."

"I was out cold and bleeding. As I'm known to do." says Jim. "So I don't remember anything."

"He was moaning a lot," remembers Darcie, who was in the car ahead. "Falling in and out of consciousness. We kept saying his name over and over again: 'Jim Guthrie, are you okay? You're going to be okay.' He kept saying 'I hurt

---

19 Pipe Street Studio, where Evan Gordon would be the one pressing record, saw more than its fair share of bands come through it too.

20 A name taken from a brand of crumby, soft shell guitar cases.

real bad,' and his one eye was just going crazy. The side of his face got smashed."

"He has a plate in there," Colin chimes in. "Titanium."

"His appearance changed." Darcie laughs some. "The hair cut stayed the same."

"Shortly after that he moved out [of his parent's house]," says Colin. "That was huge. For him to change locations, it's a big deal. Jim doesn't move much. Even though it was the same city, it was a big deal."

James Ogilvie—who, with his sister Nancy, played as The Tidbits, was a bassist in By Divine Right for a spell, and appears on *The Goods* with The Valentines—moved in shortly thereafter. Like Jim, James was disinterested in college and had put school money towards turning the basement into a recording studio.

"The environment itself was pretty dingy," remembers Jordan Howard, now enlisted as a shredder in Jim's baseball team-sized live band, but at the time in the high school-aged Stranger Rocket, who recorded at the Roksac. "It wasn't finished. I was still living with my parents and we had a finished basement... It felt like I was going into a weird dungeon. It looked pretty sketchy. There were mouldy, musty carpets, but for me it was the coolest thing ever."

The Roksac became host, along with plenty of other unassuming, shabby houses in Guelph, to rock shows chock-a-block with "some of the craziest rock you'd ever heard."

"I would come back [from university]," says Beate, "and there'd be all these people that I didn't know, a lot of younger people, over at Jim's house. Before I left, he just had these goofy songs that we'd play together. It was super low-key.

But I'd come back and there were all these fans, and all these shows going on. Guelph was popping."

Away at school himself, Simon Osborne was getting reports back. "I was talking to Jim all the time and he was telling me about all this exciting stuff going on. Basically, he was starting his own scene. It was building up around him. Suddenly this whole town of kids, a little bit younger than him, were inspired and buying 4-tracks and doing the same thing."

On the topic of his citywide influence, Jim is characteristically humble and shruggy. "I got the feeling that people looked up to me," he says, "and I'd never felt that before. It was really special and important in a way that I didn't understand. When I was younger people would look at me because I was stuttering, doing something that I was ashamed of. And then I had this group of people who looked at me because they liked what I did, looked at me in a really kind light that I wasn't comfortable with [at first]."

Jim's humbleness isn't an act. He was never a leader, but, rather, a facilitator and a participant and essentially a peer to whomever looked up to him—playing in their bands, getting them shows, luring them into his basement. His tank full of Steve McCuen and Gord High's can-do gas, if he was leading at all, it was solely by example.

In asking Aaron Riches about his relationship with Jim, a relationship that had them playing borrowed instruments for two people in Baltimore, to touring the U.K. as part of the Rough Trade roster, what sticks out most to him is just one random time he swung by the Roksac.

"I went to Russia in 1996," he recalls, "and before I went, I stopped by Jim's. I guess he was 4-tracking some stuff. I don't really remember all of why I went there. We played some music, Jim made a curry... There might've been other people there. It's very foggy to me. But I remember that it was more important to get together, than it was [to make the music]. If it all worked out, and the sound was good, great. But that was for somebody else to worry about. The real beauty, for us, was just getting together. At Jim's house, at the Roksac, making the curry and smoking a cigarette on the back porch was as important as the music being played.

"The thing is, that the music was not that important was what made the music *so* important. Because then the music—at least, from our point of view—became a testament, or a witness, to the experience we were sharing."

While a serious amount of blood was pumping to Guelph's DIY extremities, the established music scenes and the industry itself in Canada were atrophying. Kids like me all over the country were hocking their Age of Electric, Rusty, and Corky and the Juice Pigs CDs.

"I don't know why something that had thrived for decades suddenly dried up. Part of it was a glut," surmises music critic Michael Barclay, "a lowering of standards. Everyone could be a band, so everyone was a band. Therefore, there were a lot of shitty bands.

"I came of a generation," he says, "where it seemed feasible to have a half-decent life as a musician, to have enough avenues available to you, and those all fell out in the 90s."

It's a whole different scummy hot tub of reasons why the music industry shit the bed. Whether it was glut, or major labels focusing their energy on breaking indie bands in the

States and abandoning them when they couldn't, or bars replacing bands with DJs—whatever the reason, the feasibility of making a half-decent living vanished.

"I found myself broke and bitter," says Barclay, who played keys with Black Cabbage. While not a huge cash generator, the band managed to tour the country successfully. Not long after the group folded, so did *Id Magazine*, the indie biweekly Barclay had been writing for. "I don't think anyone knew what to do with the music business. Nowhere to play, no money to make. There didn't seem to be a goal.

"There was nothing else to do but go to the basement. It was a perfect time for someone like Jim, or Royal City, to thrive. A few years earlier they would've just been lost in the shuffle."

Though the release of *A Thousand Songs* was the beginning of something for me, it was sort of the end of something for Guelph. When I started to go downtown for reasons other than getting my ears lowered, that specific wave of rock was about to break. Inevitably there's that moment, in any thriving scene, when you start to notice people you've never seen before showing up to see bands you thought only you knew about. Maybe I was that kid you look at and say, "What's Ass Crack doing here?" The fact that I had a CD case with four discs in it that I felt comfortable calling Guelph Music suggests that things were beginning to congeal. And as soon as you can put your finger on what's special about a thing, other people can put their hands on it too.

In some ways, Jim couldn't help but become a figurehead of this time, this place, this sound. With The Eruption, he had a major hand in constellating that random spill of musicians and bands. And maybe it's convenient to tie the end of that generation of music to Jim leaving Guelph, but that was the general feeling at the time.

"For some people," says Stewart Gunn, "the little world of our home rock cassettes was the biggest thing, and that's what people were listening to. There're certain musical characteristics that have become 'Guelph' characteristics. Having played together over the last 15 years, there's this commonality that came out of that, this feedback loop of things being created and then consumed directly by a small group of people, which would fuel another creation. The limitations that that imposed means that there are certain musical elements I guess you could say are sort of a 'Guelph Sound.'

"Knowing Jim, being able to discern that he did have some level of skill or talent, or whatever you want to call it, that the rest of us didn't, certainly made me interested in how he did that. So I tried to parse what he does that I don't. And I figured out that he listens to a lot of music that doesn't sound anything like the music he makes," Stewart explains. "Whereas I was listening to Smog and Sebadoh and Beck—all white guys who are 25 sitting in a basement with a 4-track—it's sort of like a photocopy of a photocopy. You're losing resolution instead of going to the source.

"I remember Jim talking about J.S. Bach, and he had [read a] short biography—it was actually a kid's book. It was this disarming moment [for me]. Here was this guy, who was 25, who just read this kid's book because it seemed cool. There was something just really human about that moment. But it also speaks to the idea of broadening these musical horizons, and wanting to know what this dead composer was doing 300 years before and trying to bring some of what he was doing into 1996.

"A lot of times, that's where the really special things in life stand out, is when someone looks beyond their own limited horizons."

Riding a momentum with Royal City and the gradual rise of Three Gut Records, Jim, then 27, finally left for Toronto in the winter of 2000. "I stayed way too long," he says.

In his interview with *Wavelength*, conducted barely a half a year after he'd split, Jim expressed a lucid awareness of the change: "Things still seem to be happening these days" he wrote, "but it's not as condensed and it's a little less innocent. Not that everybody's scrambling to get on the front cover of *Now* magazine, I don't think that was ever anybody's intention. Looking back, it was just friends making music for friends and realizing our own individual potential. Now there's only a handful of the same people making music with the intention of reaching more people outside of our community. I think we all feel pretty fortunate that we are able to take those past experiences and let them fuel our art now, and in the future."

CHAPTER 3

The Royal City All-Stars

"The most beautiful things in life are given accidentally."
– Aaron Riches

A Thousand Songs opens with an accident. Jim makes it as far as the first line—"Think I'll write a thousand songs today..."—before his gear slides off the table, landing in a muffled feedback squeal and crash[21].

A Thousand Songs skims the cream off Jim's four Sonic Bunny tapes, but reducing it to a "Best Of" would be a mistake. Nearly a quarter of the jam-packed disc is new material, and the newbies—mature, thoughtful, funky, instrumental in a way Jim won't seriously return to until 2011's *Sword & Sworcery LP*—shuffle his oldies into something grander than

---

21 "I didn't own a mic stand," says Jim, "and had to lay/prop mics up with books and dirty socks. Shit was always falling over, but that time the mic rolled off the table and the cord pulled some other shit down along with it."

their origins. *A Thousand Songs* is not a Best Of, but an album that took about a decade to make.

It's maybe convenient to connect the strides in sensibility that Jim took between 1995's *Home Is Where The Rock Is* and '96's *Victim of Lo-Fi* to his being blown out of his shoes, nearly dying, and gaining a fresh outlook on and appreciation for life, but the first sound on that next tape is literally the sound of strides. A field recording of walking through leaves opens *Victim*, the rhythm of the swish and crinkle suggesting the walker's heading somewhere, not in a rush, but not taking their time either.

"Jim wasn't really able to enjoy the fall that year," Darcie Clark points out about the autumn of '95. "He loves the fall, so that really bummed him out."

There's still youthful screaming and cacophony and poopy jokes[22], but there's also this growing patience and curiosity for life's minutiae—or at least the sound of life's minutiae. On these early tapes Jim calibrates a radar that allows him to register an impressive depth in tiny, handy things—be they sounds or silences. Though his second album, there are audible hints of how Jim will sound 20 years later.

"One of the things about home rock," says Aaron Riches, "and with Jim's approach to music, was it celebrated the contingency of making music. It really allowed that magic, that happening, to be at the forefront. It wasn't very controlling."

When it's done right, lo-fi's real triumph is the allowance it makes for things you can't control. Take "Roads and Paper Routes," a nostalgic slow-burner from '97s *Docu-*

---

22 The swirl and gurgle of a toilet flushing briefly joins the fall walk.

menting Perks. During the lead guitar take, Jim's home phone rings[23]. As he gets up to answer it, the song waits. In the background there's the Doppler of cars passing in the street and screaming babble of school kids[24]. If you listen, you can hear Jim tap a finger on his guitar body, counting the other tracks in, and all the Jim's pick up where they left off. I could lay down some nipple foam, pack in some snacks, and spend a long weekend inside that moment. It's documented mostly because Jim didn't want to rewind and re-record. But it survives because Jim knows a good accident when he hears one.

If Lou Barlow's self-described "stinking garden of delights" is an apt sack to tie up the early days of Guelph home rock in, the next, Chicago-based wave of influence might well be called a carefully clipped topiary. I don't keep up with classifications, but apparently "post-rock" is the preferred nomenclature for the sort of unhurried, progressive-y rock that enveloped the city in the late 90s. This post-rock stuff has a gentle, sometimes repetitive pace that was choice for Jim's burgeoning inclusion of smaller, calmer nuances. But Jim was never precious with a genre often defined by preciousness, never shy about taking it apart and seeing how it works on these albums. Throughout this rarely juvenile juvenilia, Jim doesn't simply reassemble his influences—classic rock, home rock, post-rock, pop and poop culture—he

---

23 Mark Goldstein reminded me of John Fahey's "Poor Boy," where Fahey's dog interrupts the take by barking, and Fahey stops to shush the thing.

24 The Rocsak is directly across from the now closed Tytler PS. Jim would attach a mic to the screen window to get their ruckus, and the screaming of those squirts can be found throughout many of his tunes.

confidently Frankenstein's them into structures that are animated by an energy that's irrefutably his.

A Thousand Song's introductory accident isn't so much a sign of disaster as it is of fragility—scraping a thumb on the knife's edge that a lot of these tracks live on, sonically as well as musically. As an introduction to five and a half years of Three Gut Records, which flew pretty far and high by the seat of its pants, it's perfect. But of course, it's also just a joke. Jim sets out to write a thousand songs, but doesn't get any further than pointing for the fences before he's beaned.

We're dallying in the vestibule of the pre-Millenium here, before being ushered into the big old many-roomed, porn-filled house of the internet. Reaching beyond your own base and grabbing people with anything resembling a firm grip was slow going. Jim's first break out of Guelph was being featured on Brave New Waves, the premiere late-night source for some of the best, far flung music you'd never heard.

"To hear Patti [Schmidt's] iconic voice rattling off my name and song title was a huge thrill," says Jim, who would listen to the show during his night shifts. "I shit my pants."

"I certainly remember when *A Thousand Songs* came in," says Patti. "I didn't know Jim, I didn't know the scene in Guelph. One of the great things about Brave New Waves, there was never a programming committee, there was never any directives from the CBC. The mandate was certainly fluid and able to cope with the death of alternative rock and the popularization of indie rock. We always managed to find a rich underground and were never stuck in any particular identity genre. It was all innocent discovery.

"'Who Needs What' was a big favourite. I think that's the one that I played the most. There was definitely something about my personal aesthetic at the time. It's kinda of *de rigueur* now, that kind of toy sound, bedroom folk thing—it's been almost beaten to death—but it was still charming then. And it showed really great songwriting chops on Jim's part, great vocal presentation—not affected or shticky. It was an incredible surprise, and an incredible, modest record. It was one of my favourites that year."

"When he made that album, I don't know what his goal was," says Beate, "aside from making music. At the time he was on welfare, shoplifting Patak's curry paste from Zhers and getting a cheap loaf of bread to make 'curry toast.' I don't think he thought that album would be big and popular. But it was. I think he was a bit surprised. He was sort of toiling away, famous with us, and then *A Thousand Songs* came out, and other people liked it too."

"I put out that album in August of 1999," says Jim, "around a year or more before [Three Gut] was legit. I asked Tyler [Clarke Burke] to help me lay out the art and while hanging out for that, I told her a story about how kids used to call me 'Jimmy Threeguts,' which she thought was a hoot. I had a few other crappy names for a fake label and when it came time to put a name on the art Tyler suggested 'Three Gut Records.' She even designed the logo. I never did 'label things' and never had any intentions of running a label. It was just a name and a logo on the back of a CD that didn't sell more than a few hundred copies. It wasn't until *At Rush Hour the Cars* came out that Tyler and Lisa [Moran] took over and kicked some ass."

A Rheostatics fan, Lisa Moran came to Guelph to work for the DROG label. Through her gig there, she met Aaron Riches. The two albums that he'd released with DROG— *Over The Light Post* (1995) and *Rain* (1998)—were fairly traditional folk, up the earnest political alleys of Woody Guthrie and Pete Seeger, but shot from a similar hip as his hardcore efforts. For Aaron's third record, he and Lisa kicked around the possibility of going in another direction, label-wise.

Aaron himself was moving in a new direction. Royal City fans might not recognize the voice on the '95 and '98 albums. The vocals are deep, hearty, and announced, delivered so anyone not interested in listening will at least hear them. "After *Rain*, though," says Michael Barclay, "Aaron fell in love with Will Oldham's early recordings and older hillbilly music." Aaron began to let his voice break and lilt in emulation, and his songwriting, too, became more delicate. Those early Royal City songs shared Jim's interest in small details, in the poetry of the banal–if not in approach, certainly in spirit. The Roksac, smelling of curry and cigarettes, made for an ideal place to record this third album.

"Aaron was purging a lot of his own shit from the hardcore scene," says Simon Osborne. "He was really committed to the idea of writing simple songs and it being a little shitty. Like, he wanted this small, broken sound."

Accompanied by Evan Gordon—son of Guelph folk cornerstone James Gordon—Aaron had been playing live under the name Royal City[25] for a spell. A version of *At Rush Hour*

---

25 Maybe a subconscious, if not overt, reference to Palace. It was also, Aaron agrees, a wink to The Royal City Home Rock Eruption.

the Cars was recorded, but lost thanks to the magnetic unreliability of the VHS-like A DAT technology. For the second pass, Simon Osborne and drummer Nathan Lawr were invited over. "I was barely involved in that first record," says Simon. Royal City wasn't really a band then, just a name; it was Aaron Riches featuring the Jim Guthrie Quintet. The Royal City All-Stars, as they were known for a while.

Not long before *A Thousand Song*'s release, The Jim Guthrie Quintet was assembled. The band included Simon, Nathan, Evan, and James Ogilvie. "People in Guelph thought it was cool," remembers Nathan, "and we'd had a few Toronto forays, but it wasn't the same splash."

"I'd seen Jim playing without any context," says journalist Stuart Berman. "There were 10 people in Lee's Palace, everyone was seated, which is a pretty barren experience. At the time I just thought, 'Oh, here's someone going for a Sea and Cake kinda vibe.' it was nice and pleasant, but I didn't think that much of it at the time."

The Quintet didn't last long. "I think confrontation and saying what he wanted was hard for Jim," recalls Simon. "He doesn't want to be the centre of attention on stage, but he's the centre of his music. [The Quintet] did this aborted recording session and there was some intra-band friction for a few different reasons[26], and then it just fizzled. That was about the time Royal City started. And Royal City was the perfect way [for Jim] to let that steam off, and he kept making music on his own anyway."

The band was still an idea as much as it was a band, de-

---

26 All water under the bridge.

fined by sparseness, necessity. Maybe the best articulation of this—other than the music itself—is Tyler's album art for *At Rush Hour The Cars*. The top third of the white cover features rough outlines of a band, below that the band name and album title jotted down like a phone message, and, below that, just negative space.

Early Royal City shows could be trying. They were a quiet band that expected you to listen. It wasn't unheard of for Aaron to demand attention and respect from the audience, or just bark at them. "Royal City shows were pretty fucking precious," laughs Nathan Lawr.

"Royal City was divisive," says Barclay, "which Aaron loved. Great art is not something you can ignore easily. And the thing with Royal City being divisive, is the people who loved them really loved them. And it's very attractive to love something other people don't understand. It gives you, the audience member, some sense of exclusivity."

"The first year of [Three Gut] was a conspiracy," Aaron told Barclay[27]. "Nothing less than that." The initial conception was for a "crazy anarchist collective," but it didn't take long for the larger vision and clerical work to land in the laps of Tyler and Lisa. "No one gave a shit about any of the bands on the label at that point. If it was a conspiracy mainly between me and my punk rock ideas of the past, it was also that Tyler had this quacky, crazy art thing, and Lisa had this unbelievable fidelity to the people she had worked with and to making music happen... Then Jim had this whole home rock thing. It was a

---

27 In 2005, Barclay conducted an oral history of Three Gut for *Exclaim!*.

combination of all those things that gave it a spirit."

But as people were giving an increasing shit about the label and its bands, it made sense for Jim to grow along with it, to get out of Guelph. "I don't know if I would have moved to Toronto [if not for Royal City]," he told Barclay. "It was a really big part of my growth. There's no doubt I would have made music the whole time. But for sure, the label and all the people involved had everything to do with all the places I've been. It's given me a life I wouldn't have had."

Doing no favours to the growing idea that the label was some Guelph cabal, a handful of those involved all shared a house like an indie rock Monkees. The Three Gut House is the last in a string of row houses in the Queen West area, a bit dumpy, but still humble. "It was a halfway house for Guelph people," says Simon. Members of King Cobb Steelie were the first in, and Aaron joined at the close of the 90s. When Jim moved in, he took a room that would fail to meet the legal standards of "a room."

"That house used to a be a convent," says Aaron, "and I'm sure that the room Jim was in had been a pantry. There were no windows. But it was bigger than a closet. We called it the beer closet because that's where we used to put the old beer bottles. After a party, all the empties would go into this terrible room. There were probably dead rats in there. It was awful. Then when Jim moved to Toronto, we took all the dead rats and all the beer bottles out. The empties went down to the basement after that. But then Jim cleaned that up at some point, and [Royal City] would practise down there."

Jim's rent fluctuated depending on the number of people coming in and out of the house, but was always low enough for him to focus on music, whether on the road with Royal City, or on his own in the beer closet.

"That bedroom was such a little shit hole," laughs Stephen Evans. "Jim didn't go to university, and he had shitty jobs, and he did so much with the little money he had. He lived in that pantry for years, and that's where he really took off. He built this amazing little studio in that shit hole of a room and he made some amazing music in that dank hole."

"Jim always put his music before anything," Nathan explains. "Before girls, before fashion, before diet. He's just invested in it. Kinda unflinchingly. He lived in that closet not because he didn't care, but [because] it was gonna be cheaper, and he could just do his music."

A benefit of the type of work that Jim was doing was how little space it required. In the insert of *A Thousand Songs*, along with shots of a condiment-heavy fridge, disembodied piano keys, a lock in a door chipped away at by key stabs, is a mote-filled shot of Jim's Fostex 4-track perched on his knees. The machine's so tiny, balanced there like a house cat not sure whether it's going to settle down or hop off. It might not occur to you that this dude had just stuffed a wealth of wacky, wise stuff into that little container that you could so easily whip against a wall and destroy. And while Jim's bedroom pop trajectory followed the path of a generation's worth of budding musicians, he took an uncanny turn when he stopped to pick up the *MTV Music Generator* for PlayStation, a tiny console that slides just perfectly into a nun's pantry.

"It's basically a sequencer, synthesizer, and recording program," Jim told author and Hand Eye Society founder

Jim Munroe in 2004. "You have 24 tracks, and a bunch of sounds. A whole bunch of different loops. If you don't know how to make music, you can pick from these prefab beats, kind of cut-and-paste, paint-by-numbers, and when you put it together it's all in the same key so it all works together magically. It's really not a game at all, it's more of a program. You can also take a CD and sample three or four seconds, and what I do is make my own drums and burn it to CDs and put myself in the game.

"It just made sense with some of the songs I was doing to get that synth sound from the PlayStation. A lot of the synth songs for the older video games are really brilliant. The Moogy, analog sounds. With the music I get from the PlayStation, it's a texture I'm going for sonically to achieve certain emotions."

"It does have a dorky sound," he told *Exclaim!* in 2002, "but the real challenge is trying to milk something natural out of it."

It was alone in that limited space, with that limited technology, that Jim started to articulate those synthetic textures that, a decade later, would make the *Sword & Sworcery LP* such a sonic corker. And when he began to lay the foundations for the *Morning Noon Night* and *Now, More Than Ever* material, it was with the PlayStation. But simultaneously, Royal City was turning from a project into a band, Three Gut from a conspiracy into a movement.

"I've always maintained that Three Gut bands, and Royal City especially, were the first non-hardcore bands to make that foray [into the U.S].," says Nathan Lawr. "We weren't a punk band, but that's no reason for us—and this was really

Tyler's thinking—not to do it. It was that period of the internet where it was still kind of amazing."

"Early on in the label we saw Billy Bragg's manager speak," says Lisa Moran, "and he said something to the effect that when you're starting out you can break all the rules, because you don't know what they are and that's the best time. But since things change constantly there aren't really rules."

A quick dip into the States, during a time when Leslie Feist was sitting in on guitar, was followed by a more burly Feist-less, Jim-full three-week tour. "Crossing the border was kinda doable," says Nathan. Of course, we're talking the twilight of the pre-9/11 border. As doable as border crossing might have been then, Royal City was still turned away, sent home with permission to come back without their instruments. So the band cancelled the show they had booked in Philadelphia that night, regrouped[28], and resumed, instrument-less.

"The yin to that yang," says Nathan, "our first show was in Baltimore: we show up, and we're like, 'We're really sorry, Other Bands, but we don't have any instruments. Can we borrow yours?' Simon had to play a five string fretless bass, Jim had to play this neon green Samick, Steve Vai guitar, and the drum kit was up on this big riser. That was our first show of the tour. It was fucking hilarious.

"In the wake of this shit show, Sarah Harmer asked us to open up for her on her Canadian tour."

Sarah had caught Royal City in Nashville, October 2000. "I remember being really happy to socialize with some Cana-

---

28 Insult to injury, they returned home to a devastating *Magnet* review of At Rush Hour The Cars.

dian musicians," she says, "and really dug their music and poster and T-shirt art. Their show really made me question whether I was living enough on the edge."

The following spring, Royal City joined Sarah on tour, playing from Vancouver to Winnipeg. In Jim's 20-year career, he's never played live as much as he did with Royal City.

"I'm not sure how many shows The Quintet actually played," says Aaron. "I mean, when we were living it, it felt like they had played tons of shows, but I think they probably only played 12 ever. What happened with Royal City was we played twice that many shows on one tour. There wasn't any pressure on Jim to be the performer. He just exploded as a guitar player. I'm not sure the records he made after would've been the same if he'd never played in Royal City. Not because Royal City was a great band, but because it gave Jim a freedom to play guitar in a way he'd never played before."

Aaron describes *At Rush Hour the Cars* as "kind of a slow moving picture of a band being born."

"By the time we made *Alone at the Microphone*," he says, "we were a band. Most of those songs, by the time we recorded them had been played live, a lot."

Everyone involved hit an unprecedented stride on that album, but Jim comes especially alive. From the howling solo indistinguishable from actual screams on "Bad Luck," to the janky wanking on "Spacey Basement," Jim's guitar becomes as much a character as an instrument on that album. "That was his first major Guitar Hero moment," says Simon. "I remember thinking 'Where's this stuff coming from?' Seriously. He did the solo for 'Spacey Basement' and

I remember going nuts. There was a space for it, and we all thought Jim would do a mediocre solo, but he pulled a Neil Young on us. We didn't know where it came from. He got so many pats on the back for that he was probably like, 'I'm just gonna keep going with this.'"

Released in 2002, *Alone at the Microphone* blew everyone's hair back, critics and fans both. Sparse, haunted, full of meat and cigarettes, dappled with shit and blood and a miscellany of other fluids, there's nothing else like that album in tone and execution, and—for my money—dramatic structure. Never mind sound, in terms of ebullient prowess, that album slots in perfectly with the confident, seminal-feeling music that came out of Toronto at the turn of the century. The Hidden Cameras *Smell of Our Own*, Constantines' self-titled, and *Alone at the Microphone* are shots in the arm, kicks in the ass, and loving, sweat-stinking embraces.

The hub of the Canadian music industry, Toronto was still reeling from the popping of that 90s bubble. "It just seemed like the excitement was gone," says Stuart Berman. "There was this moment where Toronto's version of the post-Nirvana effect, where a lot of Toronto bands were getting big record contracts, and were suddenly on Much-Music a lot. Around '97 or '98, it became clear that these bands weren't gonna be the next Nirvana and it seemed like a cycle had come to an end.

"The Guelph influx was definitely felt. The Three Gut crew brought this different kind of sensibility and energy which coincided with things that were [starting] to happen, with Broken Social Scene and Wavelength, which was a big, galvanizing force."

There was a feeling that these new bands, new labels, new venues "were forging a new participatory culture inside and outside of Toronto clubs," Berman writes in *This Book Is Broken*, "staging concerts in warehouse lofts, galleries, and churches and cross-pollinating with local art, activist, and queer communities. Within this open environment, the primary motivation for playing music was not a contract but simply contact: shared ideas, collaborations, audience interaction."

In 2000, Stuart became editor of *Eye Weekly*. "We had Royal City on the cover. That was for the release show for *At Rush Hour the Cars*. And then the Three Gut T-shirts started appearing around town and it seemed like Tyler and Lisa were really creating a nice little scene there. People like Feist were being drawn into it—I know she was a really big Jim Guthrie fan. Tyler and Lisa were great at casting the net wider than core indie rock people. They were getting great press from outlets that wouldn't normally cover something like that, because they had an artistic vision. They crossed over with the art scene and the media scene who were always looking for something to write about."

But if Three Gut was setting up the ball, it was The Hidden Cameras who spiked the thing. "They were a real force of nature," says Stuart. "That was the band where I felt, at that time, 'This could become something really big.' Whereas, initially, Royal City and Jim Guthrie were maybe a little too low-key to grab people, The Hidden Cameras came barrelling out like a clown car with people all over the stage, dancing and playing glockenspiels. And the songs were amazing.

"In the 90s," says Stuart. "Canadian bands weren't getting written about in *Spin*, or the *NME*, or any U.S. or U.K. publications of note, and those were the driving tastemakers, that was your key to having a career and being able to tour there. In the early 2000s that started to crumble."

After the Cameras, it's safe to say that the Constantines were the next galvanizing force. Though not complete strangers, the Cons were the first "outside" band to be signed to Three Gut—a deal struck over a spaghetti dinner. Certainly, a shot in the arm to Royal City, who had stayed seated. Music could still be precious without being *precious*. The Cons brought an intelligence and an energy to rock that made for a skeleton key good for opening up theretofore closed audiences.

International interest in what some might now call Torontopia came thanks to the Cameras, who caught the attention of Geoff Travis and Rough Trade Records, becoming the first Canadian band signed to that label, followed soon by the Cons signing to Sub Pop. And it was in this round of courting that Royal City's hand likewise got taken by Rough Trade.

If you're reading this hot off the presses, we're nearing the 10th anniversary of the shuttering of Three Gut Records. The label's legacy is a difficult one to dig through, not on account of there being a tangle of finely tooled, tiny moving parts in there, but because the simplicity of its guts belies the range of its effect and influence.

"The goal" says Lisa Moran, "was to get people to listen to the music that my friends were making that I loved."

Three Gut was a label because they said they were. But the thing with influence is it doesn't matter so much what a thing actually is, but how it seems. If Three Gut were making things up as they went along, that's not how it appeared. So when other upstarts–Arts and Crafts, say–set out to do their own thing, the directionless direction of Three Gut was the way they went.

Around 2003, Tyler started to shift focus to her own art, leaving Lisa to keep all the plates spinning.

"I could sense, at the time of Three Gut's dissolution, that Tyler and Lisa's heads were at different places," says Stuart. "They weren't putting out as many records, their biggest bands were on other labels internationally, and people like Reg and Jim didn't cross over to the same extent that they'd hoped for. It was maybe more a sign of the times than an out-of-nowhere tragic event. It was a beautiful thing, but all beautiful things have to end eventually. And if their hearts weren't in it the same way they used to be, then it's probably best to put it down."

Three Gut is gigantic in my own memory, my own experience, and it's strange to think that it was just something that happened for five years. A bunch of lovely, honest people did a bunch of lovely, honest things when they were in the same place at the same place together. Though maybe the upside of that core simplicity is, like a beheaded turtle, Three Gut's workings were so simple that the thing still looks like it's moving all these years later.

Little Heart's Ease, the first album Royal City released jointly with Rough Trade and Three Gut would be their last—not counting a memorial B-sides that came out in 2010 on Sufjan Steven's Asthmatic Kitty label. If *Alone at the*

Microphone was obsessed with death, *Little Heart's Ease* celebrated life. It's an album of feasts, and marriage, and cleanliness. Maybe bothered by the lack of *Alone*'s feces, critics shit all over *Little Heart's Ease*. It's a shame, too, because while *Ease* isn't the best album ever, it suggests a new direction for the band, a direction that, given another album or two, might have yielded another face burner.

An autopsy reveals numerous causes for Royal City's croaking: the album's poor reception, Aaron's pursuit of academics, Nathan Lawr splitting for Vancouver, the moving away of the remaining members. But this is all just baubles hanging off the fact that the band wasn't built for long hauls.

"Royal City was best when it didn't have a project," explains Aaron.

"We were the same chuckleheads," says Simon of their growing success. "That was part of the problem. [Rough Trade] quickly realized that we didn't have a market edge. They liked our record, but we were just a bunch of doofuses. We had no game."

"It wasn't always easy and magical," Aaron goes on, "but in retrospect I don't think any one of us would change any of it. I'm grateful that I got to spend that time with those people, because we were great friends. And still are great friends."

Jim agrees: "We didn't make any money, but we didn't care, because we were getting drunk every night with our best friends." To have this dynamic change, to elevate Royal City beyond their being friends in a band, was to subject it to elements it really wasn't built to withstand.

The burden and the gift of having a long view is that the roll of randomness, of luck and chance, gets larger and larger.

The existence of Royal City is thanks to the destruction of one recording session, thanks to some phone calls made in support of another stab. That anything would grow out of that is in itself astounding.

"The most beautiful things in life are given accidentally," says Aaron. "You met this person, an event happened, and it was beautiful. In retrospect you have to cherish that because it was the most important thing that happened in your life. But it was never something you set out to do. It was something that happened to you. I think that's the case with Royal City."

That's also the case with Jim, whose career has been a balance of being lucky, palling around with good people, and working hard. But the reason you're reading a book about Jim Guthrie and not one about Royal City is Jim's talent for making good use of accidents, his talent for riding the randomness without getting bucked. The best thing about the collapse of Jim's gear at the opening of *A Thousand Songs* is the fact that 23 songs come afterwards.

CHAPTER 4

An Obvious Sense

"Jim's always just one step ahead of people, unfortunately."
– Stuart Berman

Morning Noon Night opens with a chopped up, stuttering beat of sampled drums, on top of which starts to accrue a mostly synthetic, PlayStation noise collage of cranks and whistles and pings. Spit sounds sail from the left to right channel, and the more they move, the more they seem to be caroming around in your own skull. Here and there the seemingly random reports will swoop in the same pattern, but just briefly before falling back out of order. Then, in the left ear, a crunchy chord is struck and held on a guitar, like a teacher hollering to settle a rowdy class. The guitar's interruption of this PlayStation melee nicely sums up the two dominating, sometimes conflicting interests at work on Jim's first proper album.

Released November 2002, it sounds like Royal City[29] jostled

---

29 Jim is referred to as "Royal City's Jim Guthrie" in most contemporary reviews.

loose some guitar joy. The spurts of shredding in songs like "Evil Thoughts," "Virtue," and "Days I'll Need Off" feel like siblings of the work Jim did and the sound he got on *Alone at the Microphone*. It can get dirty and shrill, and when the guitar rises and meets Jim's voice—which, when it gets up there, can get nasally in all the right ways—it's difficult to distinguish the two. The organic-sounding double helix of voice and guitar suits the synthetic, sometimes "dorky" Play-Station samples. These songs give a pretty good idea of what the old Jim Guthrie Quintet sounded like before dissolving into Royal City, and the whole gang makes an appearance on "Days I'll Need Off" and "1901[30]." Killers though those tracks may be, it's stuff like "3am" and "Houndz Of Love," quieter, more acoustic, that, like some love tester, really registers Jim's tightening grip on songcraft.

Morning Noon Night is a hell of a pop album. "3am," "Houndz," and "1901" are the sort of hop, skip, and jump that will land Jim into *Now, More Than Ever* territory. But compositions like the head-fucky opener, "In The Hour of Her Sore Need," and two later instrumental tracks, "Toy Computer" and "Right and Right Again," are sallies in the opposite direction. Both acoustically and synthetically, Jim's learning to express musically what the pop song can't.

"I've dabbled in both songs and instrumental music since day one," says Jim. "People always responded to the songs more. And while that was encouraging, it made my relationship with my instrumental stuff feel like it was an uglier half-brother that people didn't like as much, but I was just

---

30 The only survivor of that flopped studio session in 2000.

as excited by my instrumental experiments. When anybody would comment on an instrumental song on any of my tapes or CDs, it really made me proud."

"I would like to put out one instrumental record that's like the score for some weird movie that doesn't exist," Jim told Allan Wigney in the *Ottawa Sun* before bringing *Morning Noon Night* to the capital. "But it's hard to say whether you could sit through it."

Morning finds Jim rocking out at a sort of crossroads. The arrival of *Now, More Than Ever* a year later implied that Jim took the pop road, and when that album wasn't followed up, people assumed he'd gotten lost along the way. But Jim took both roads. The promise of the singer-songwriter chops on display in this 2002 album were gratified right away; the promise of Jim as composer, as a guy who could transform dorky, video game noises into breathing, evocative sounds, would take about a decade to be fulfilled.

To hawk his new wares, Jim took his PlayStation on the road. The live set-up featured, like *Morning* itself, Jim and his guitar next to the console and a TV. The tracks he'd built were stored on memory cards, but the space was limited. After two or three songs, he'd have to switch out cards, which would take about two minutes to load. Great live theatre this was not.

"The PlayStation was me trying to play solo and I was sort of hiding behind it," Jim says. "I've never thought of myself as a singer-songwriter and always struggled with filling the room with only my voice and guitar."

"It was [also] born out of necessity," Jim told Wigney. "I didn't have the chance to get a live band together. It's a neat idea, but it's hard to have it work out live"

Classmates at University of Toronto classical music program, Mike Olsen and Owen Pallett started coming around the Three Gut HQ for Hidden Cameras rehearsals. "I met Jim around that time," remembers Mike, who got his foot firmly in the Three Gut door in 2002, joining Gentleman Reg last minute for a cross-country tour. Jim was just hanging around, in his closet.

"Jim was like, 'Oh, hey. I was wondering if you and Owen wanted to play on some recordings I've got. That'd be pretty cool.' He might've given me a 100 bucks or something. Owen and I were becoming a little bit known at that point. We were almost sort of a team. We're on about 15 records from that time. Of course, soon Owen would rocket past me like a starship," Mike laughs.

Recorded in the beer closet, Mike lends cello noodling on parable-y "Turn Musician" and both he and Owen add a swelling urgency to "Days I Need Off."

"You can kinda hear the Three Gut house in a lot of those recordings," says Mike. "That creaky piano that's never in tune is so part of his sound. He had two particular microphones—really unsuited for recording. He did all his vocals on this weird [Pressure Zone Microphone], which looked like a big square plate—he bought it from Radio Shack. They're great. But they're not for vocals. He's said before, 'It was super trebly, and sounded terrible, but I kinda liked it.' That's his sound—incredibly trebly, but also really mellow.

"The early Guthrie sound, it was lo-fi, but you could hear so much detail. There's a lot of grit in everything, and you can hear the detail in his voice. I think that served him well. He managed to do pretty subtle things, while still sounding—pardon the expression—kinda crappy. It sounded close. It became quite intimate. That was part of the charm."

To pull off *Morning Noon Night* in the flesh, Jim hung onto Mike and Owen, had Simon handy, and—with Nathan Lawr living in Vancouver—brought Evan Clarke aboard on drums.

"We might've rehearsed once or twice with the *Morning Noon Night* band," says Mike. "I didn't know those guys, Evan and Simon. They could be like the Constantines[31,] sort of cagey and anti-social. Those first rehearsals felt weird. I didn't know if it was going to be any good.

"But then we went to Ottawa and played Babylon[32] and as soon as we hit the stage, it was fucking dynamite. I'd played with Owen, so I knew that part was going to be fine. The strings were really hot in that band; they weren't just a gesture. That was a rock band with an integrated string section that was not a quiet sound. We were aggressive, and the rhythm section was loud and pounding, yet the sounds were quite sensitive. We were doing the *Morning Noon Night*, transforming the video game material into strings."

The tour carried on to Montreal. I saw that show at the Jupiter Room with a Unitarian classmate who was giving a white cowboy hat a lamentable whirl that evening. Opening for Jim were these kids also sporting queer headgear—motorcycle helmets—called Arcade Fire. Jim's band was eager and raucous—huffing some residual energy, maybe, from the sometimes confrontational Arcade Fire set—a far cry

---

31 Yup, Mike also spent some time with the Cons
32 January 18, 2003

from the gentle rocking builds of The Quintet. It was the first time I'd seen Jim play standing up. The *Morning* songs likewise got out of their seats, were elevated, enlivened—the vibe specific to those five players. The Unitarian left after a few songs, complaining about the loudness, and apparently had his hat snatched off by the wind.

"Within three or four days [of the tour]," Mike says, "Jim decided that we needed to record another record with *this* band. It was already understood that this needed to be captured."

"The year between *Morning Noon Night* and *Now, More Than Ever* was a magical combo of being really productive," says Jim, "being decisive and being lucky to have surrounded myself with so many amazing people. There was also a good little buzz going around the label and spirits were high. It really makes a huge difference when you have a close-knit community of friends rooting for you. I've been lucky to have always felt that."

No one being able to see through the fog back to the Spring of 2003, I got Andy Magoffin, who recorded *Now, More Than Ever*, to check his files. He wrote back: "I have a big 'JG' down for March 1, 2, 7, 8, and 9." This stretch would have been when the bed tracks of *Now, More Than Ever* got laid down with Jim, Simon, and Evan. A "Jim" written next to March 22 and 23 suggests that this is when Mike and Owen popped by to write and record the strings.

A quick survey of the albums made in Ontario in the 2000s will yield a commonality beyond the presence of Mike Olsen and Owen Pallett: "Recorded by Andy Magoffin at the House of Miracles." Throw a dart at a college radio station's library, and you're likely to hit a Magoffin-made record.

"It was sort of a trend, I think," Andy says of this seeming ubiquity. "We were all about the same age, and these were young bands who hadn't really made records yet, and didn't know any other studios, but they knew me. So everyone played it safe and went to Andy's place because that's what their buddies did."

While a former nun's pantry is a fine place to record an album, it should be pointed out that it was thanks to a Factor grant that Jim was able to get that band into The House of Miracles. "If I hadn't got the grant it would have been a much different record," Jim says, "I was too comfortable making records in my bedroom and the grant got me off my ass [into the] studio." Much of the charm of Jim's earlier albums is a result of their being recorded in different places, at different times, each song a sort of record of its conception and execution. But to capture a sound and energy specific to a set group of players, getting into a proper studio was the thinking.

"I remember Jim saying from the outset that he wanted to make a 'small' record," says Andy. "That he wanted to make a 'modest' record. If you're working in a small studio with a small band, usually the goal is to make things sound bigger than life, larger than the pieces you have to work with. Jim didn't want that. We had to make sure there was no ambience on the drums, that everything was really dry, plain-sounding, so we killed all the reflection in the room. Didn't go after any big reverbs or anything. Then of course Owen got involved and things took a turn for the big."

"I don't know if Jim wanted a strings-record before I did

'Days I'll Need Off' or not," says Owen. "We had somewhat middling expectations, to be honest. Jim was, though we didn't know it, at the beginning of a long period of writer's block. More accurately, he just stopped writing. The songs for *Now, More Than Ever* were old, some new, but there were no other songs forthcoming. He presented to us only one new song during the year we were working together."

"I can start new songs like nobody's business," Jim cops, "but finishing them has always been a sadder affair. I've had a real aversion to it in the past. It's like every new idea is a mystery waiting to be explored and unlocked and then after a few bars the possibilities become overwhelming and I put it down and start something else. It's like I don't want to mess up this chance encounter with a real gem. It can be so many things in that moment, ya know?

"*Now, More Than Ever* was a mix of old and new ideas. At least four or five of the songs were started in the early 90s and I'd pick at them over the years, but it wasn't their time. It was intuition that dictated what songs would make up the album. It was also the grant that pushed me to finish lyrics. I can write instrumentals all day long but lyrics are tough for me. It was really important to have a deadline. Deadlines bring out the best in everyone."

The title track goes back to at least '97, where it appeared as "An Obvious Sense" on *Documenting Perks*; you'll find a proto "Save It" on *Some Things You Should Know...*; and The Quintet was playing a version of "So Small" since at least '99.

If the songs were old, the attack was fresh. "Hear this social disaster / Social, in terms of laughter" in "So Small" circa '99 becomes "So small, on a porch in Montreal / the setting sun,

Missy catches flies for fun" in '03. Musically, the two versions are basically the same, but the first version is doleful, angsty-sounding at times, whereas the version on *Now, More Than Ever* is lighter, sometimes weightless in the way it observes the world. The earlier version of the song covers a specific-sounding awkwardness—"Don't sweat the small things"—whereas the update's about being dwarfed by perception, feeling small in a world full of moments that grow bigger when you pay them the right kind of attention.

In terms of images, scenarios described, *Now, More Than Ever* is such a well-written album, comparable to *Alone at the Microphone* in its structure. It's an album about immediacy, about not wanting to get snagged by thoughts of either the past or the future, enjoying carte blanche in the immediate moment.

The idea of time is maybe the most consistent element in a seemingly scattered career. What is that interruption in "Roads and Paper Routes" if not the sound of time passing? Songs like "Jigsaw Muzzle" and "Trust" put the breaks on mid-way through, creating moments of contemplation, where the song almost seems to pause and consider itself. Structurally, Jim rarely employs the figure eight of verse-chorus-verse-chorus. Instead his songs move forward and live constantly in the present.

"I don't know what my thing with time is," Jim says, "but some days I feel like it's the only thing worth obsessing about. It really is everything. It gives and it takes. It's the ultimate equalizer. It will humble us all and I find that very comforting. Even the most cocky asshole will turn old and shitty, and I take a great pleasure in that. I'm always aware of its passing and I suppose it's my gift and my curse. Even when we think we're 'taking our time' it's time that's doing all the taking. It's life's little secret and if you can be okay with it, then I suppose it makes life more bearable."

The strings almost take on the character of time in the *Now, More Than Ever*, the swelling rush of an instant that breaks into a kind of slow motion, the way moments get sluggish when you become aware of yourself being inside of them.

"I don't think anyone expected it to be so grand," says Andy. "Owen's contribution lent the album this flare of sophistication that we weren't gonna get from the core players. I don't think Jim knew what he was getting into by asking Owen to do the arrangements."

"I'd been playing with Owen for a couple of years at this point," Jim wrote on his website for the album's 10th anniversary, "both in Royal City and my own stuff, so I knew he was good. But I wasn't fully aware of how insanely talented he was. Watching him layer track after track of (mostly improvised) violin and viola was truly jaw-dropping. At times, what he was playing made no sense and sounded very dissonant and out of synch with the music. If you can imagine hearing the string arrangement at the end of 'Lovers Do' as a solo violin, in a quiet room (as Owen wore headphones) you'd think he was trying to ruin the song. Up until that point a lot of the songs didn't have these insane strings, so I had no idea what he was trying to do. It sounded crazy, but as he and Mike layered each part it revealed itself in a way that left us all a little speechless."

"When Owen got in a sort of manic state, when he got a really great idea, he'd grab a piece of paper and write shit down," says Mike. "The end section of 'Lover's Do' was lit-erally written in 10 minutes flat. When Owen's on, he's so on. He was working off the energy of a band that kicked ass. That band was really powerful. That's why we were [in the studio] just months after Jim had released his last record.

"The strings are what made the album different; Jim's writ-ing is what made it good."

"A lot of what also makes *Now, More Than Ever* so cohesive-sounding," says Jim, "is the band and the studio. Those guys are the glue that holds those songs together. 'Dude glue,' if you will. Maybe don't quote me on that term."

In the 10 years since its release, the lily of *Now, More Than Ever* has been gilded with a "classic" status, and while the contemporary reviews were generally great, kids also had plenty of reservations at the time of its release.

"Not everyone loved the strings when it came out," wrote Jim. "Some found it a little much in contrast to my previous, (less ambitious?) home recordings. To me, it was heaven."

"There was a dissenting voice on the Toronto message boards when this album came out," Owen elaborates, "that I had 'ruined it' with my strings, which I thought was a myopic and speculative way of looking at record-making. Records don't work like that. Many clients will mix my ar-rangements low or remove them entirely if they felt like the record would be better off without them. Jim did not. He turned them up and that's his album.

"I think Jim's attitude around this record was somewhat resigned," Owen goes on. "I remember we collectively felt very ambivalent about the final product. I did too, compared to his previous records. When it got such strong critical response, it was a complete surprise to everyone. I was always enormously proud of 'All Gone' and 'The Evangelist,' but also felt exposed by the more whimsical elements, like the electrified solo on 'Save It.' Obviously, I love the record in retrospect, though I realize now that it's a record of high quality, in the traditional sense: it lacks the scrappiness, the experimentation and free-wheeling excitement of Jim's earlier material."

From *Home Is Where The Rock Is* to *Sword & Sworcery LP*, *Now, More Than Ever* stands out. It's focused in a way Jim's earlier work isn't. Its experiment is contextual, sustained, a far cry from the boundless monkeyshine of *A Thousand Songs*. At this distance from its release, the album sounds nearly infallible, brave and confident, quirky and fragile all at once. The lyrics are like nothing else, vague but specific, dense but blousy. Overall, it's a great approximation of Jim's reservation/razzmatazz balance. But it's the product of that aforementioned forking, of Jim's bifurcated chops.

But *Now, More Than Ever*, at the time and over time, reached a wider audience who had never heard Jim Guthrie before and had no comparison to make. "It's very rare that records come along and I know they'll be with me until I'm gone," says Leon West of 3 Syllables Records, which re-released the album on vinyl in 2012. "I think any album can have a profound effect on you if you listened to it enough, and allowed it to really get into your subconscious. But *Now, More Than Ever* never felt like one of those albums. I don't feel like I want to listen to it—I *need* to listen to it. This is more than music to me. It's part of the fabric of my being."

"I thought he turned out a masterpiece," says Stuart Berman. "I thought it was going to be the next record out of Toronto to get an international deal. I figured Rough Trade would scoop him up but they signed Arcade Fire instead.

"At that time, things were getting really noisy in Toronto, with Broken Social Scene and Constantines. It might've been the right time for him, but not for the rest of the population. Jim's always just one step ahead of people, unfortunately."

"There were a lot of people around in those Three Gut days that we were playing with," says Jim. "There was a Royal City show where Broken Social Scene and Arcade Fire opened up for us in Montreal[33]. Sufjan Stevens would open for us when he'd come to Toronto in the early days. I didn't really perceive it, but it seemed like we were at the forefront of our own scene. But everyone else around us blew up in a way that no one on Three Gut ever had. Everyone went on to bigger things, so the joke was, 'If you wanna be big, you should open up for a Three Gut band.' It was a real wake-up call and I think it forced everyone in the scene, and the Canadian indie scene at large, for better or worse, to redefine success."

"The official street date of the release was November 18, 2003," Jim wrote 10 years later on his website. "But, as usual, I didn't really strike while the iron was hot. I didn't tour that much for it either, but despite my best effort to undermine the release it was still warmly received by the press and was even nominated for a Juno. A lot of the credit goes to Lisa Moran and Tyler Clark Burke at Three

---

33 December 1st, 2002, La Sala Rosa.

Gut Records, who pushed the record in ways I never would have if it was left up to me. I'm also very grateful to the group of guys that helped me make this record."

"Those were—and you can write this in your book," permits Evan Clarke, "Those were some of the funnest shows I ever played. In part, because I had certain performance and managerial responsibilities in Rockets Red Glare. You couldn't get drunk for a Rockets Red Glare show. It was fairly calibrated music. But everyone was drunk for Jim Guthrie shows, and Jim was the drunkest. For his release show, I remember him walking on stage and being, 'I'm really fucked,'" Evan whispers.

But the band didn't last long. "The strings left," explains Evan, "and there were a few shows where it was just me, Jim and Simon. There was a sense that that band was done, and that's too bad."

"Jim was pretty clear," says Mike, "that the *Now, More Than Ever* band was a temporary thing. It was a time and a place and it's done."

"I felt that we never fully, fully gelled as a five-piece," says Owen, "because we were young, because Mike was an outsider, and I was, at 22, a jerk. So, reasonably, Simon and Evan never really accepted us as bandmates. I don't remember when we stopped playing together, but when I quit all my bands to save my life and take a desk job, I don't think I had to tender my resignation with Jim. We'd been waiting for new songs and they never came."

For shits, I asked Jim to imagine a world where *Now, More Than Ever* won the Juno, where he did get snapped up internationally, and turned into a worldwide big deal. "I honestly

can't," he said. "I think I would've sabotaged it somehow.
I've always found a way to find something else to do.

"I think I became aware of it [self-sabotage] about halfway through the Three Gut reign. I remember Lisa and
Tyler asking me to do interviews and things that normal
bands would want to do and I would always be like, 'Nah.'
And they'd get mad at me, like 'We're trying to *manage*
you.' And I realized that I was kind of a pain in the ass that
way. Like, the opposite of a demanding diva. Just a weirdo.
I just wasn't comfortable... I've always been introverted in
that way and struggled with things that other people might
see as a no-brainer.

"I've sort of sabotaged my own career in ways like...
being nominated for a Juno. I certainly didn't take that
lightly, but I was never like, 'Okay, how am I gonna further
my career with this?' I almost wanted to forget about it as
soon as I got back from the Juno weekend. I knew it would
look good on a resume if I ever wanted a grant, but that
was about it. I always sucked at that kinda stuff. Three Gut
was great at it, and seeing that is when I realized that I was
trying to fuck shit up for myself.

"If there was any real sabotage, it's when I intentionally
handed in that shit-sorry application for art school. I drew
something that was below what I was capable of knowing
that I wasn't going to get in. I sabotaged a career that my
parents wanted me to have, so I could have a career that *I*
wanted to have."

"Jim was never a natural," says Owen. "I mean, nobody
is, really. But some people have enough ambition to fake
it. Aaron never did, [but] he got smart and had babies and

got doctorates. Losing your musical ambition, it's going to happen to everybody sometime. There is something deeply terrifying about having all that 'potential' realized, whether it's as minor as 'an album recorded and released' or 'winning a Grammy.' Hunger inspires, success demoralizes."

The sense with *Now, More Than Ever* was that Jim had arrived somewhere, when in fact it was just another stop on the way to whoknowshwere for Jim. The problem was, Jim moved on, but the majority of Jim lovers sat with *Now, More Than Ever*, waiting for him to come back.

"I've never dealt with expectation well," Jim says, "living up to something. I think that's sort of why I've done so many different things. I was never comfortable with 'singer-songwriter,' because there's so much expectation there. There was an expectation after *Now, More Than Ever*, I guess. But for as long as it took me to make *Takes Time*, there was this perception that I'd stopped making music. But in all that time I still managed to generate quite a lot. I made so much music after I 'stopped' making music."

CHAPTER 5

I Don't Wanna Be A Rock Star

"God it's hard to be yourself / When everyone
around you thinks you're someone else."
– "Who Needs What"

"Any long term plans?" the music website Coke Machine Glow asked Jim in 2005. He had applied for the same Factor grant that had allowed him to amp up *Now, More Than Ever*, he explains, and been turned down. "It sucks," he admitted, "but it's not like I've never done a record with no budget.

"I would love to be able to quit my part-time catering job and just do music but I can't as things stand. I'm broke. I'd just love to be smart and get lucky with money and be able to buy a house or something. That's all."

At the time, following *Now, More Than Ever*'s Juno nomination, Jim was working for the George Brown House as a resident caterer, wearing "a little monkey suit... serving groups coffee and sandwiches etc." and still living in the beer closet.

"To try and remember all the odd jobs I've ever worked is really freaking me out," Jim says when I ask him to tally his employment history. "I had so many crappy jobs growing up. My parents were working class folks and they instilled a pretty good work ethic in me. I wasn't above scrubbing toilets[34]. Deep down I knew I wasn't cut out for office jobs or any sort of post-secondary educational activities, so by the time I got out of high school I was pretty comfortable with working wherever and 4-tracking in my parents' basement. Not a great life plan at the time, but who the hell knows anything when you're 18? It's been a series of well-placed baby steps [since]. Slow and steady. I've never been in any kind of rush to get anywhere. Throughout every job, and after every shift, I'd go home and make music... until staying home to make music was my job."

Freaked out though he may have been, Jim shot me his pre-2005 resume: he's done a few tours in the fast food industry (Arby's, McDonald's, the Ontario chain Wimpy's), in gas stations and car washes, heaps of dish washing jobs, clerk at a now-closed Guelph record store, newspaper delivery, and makeshift cartooning instructor to kids aged 8 to 13.

"I tried doing extra work in film and TV, but only ever landed a day on the set of *Men With Brooms*[35]. I was in the stands for the big 'curl off' at the end of the movie[36].

"And I worked with a self-proclaimed 'ruby smuggler' at the food court across from the Three Gut headquarters

---

34 See *Home Is Where The Rock Is*'s "Been Scrubbin' The Shitter"

35 59% rating on Rotten Tomatoes.

36 Freeze frames reveal no Jim in the background. I looked so you wouldn't have to.

making sandwiches and French fries. The dude smoked a ton of hash and was totally crazy. I think he was Israeli and he travelled all over the world smuggling jewels. He ended up in Canada after the smuggling went south and he opened the sandwich shop. Interesting guy but he had zero people skills and I quit after a week or two."

Royal City got a bit of cash when they signed with Rough Trade, and maybe album and T-shirts sales might yield enough to pay for a month in a pantry, but for Jim, who had banked solely on music, that income wasn't funding a real life. "Everyone else in the band had school to fall back on," he says. "But I didn't want to have anything to fall back on. I just wanted to make music."

Three Gut folded just under two years after *Now, More Than Ever*'s release, at which time those kids with the motorcycle helmets who had opened for Jim in 2003 had created such an impressive ruckus that it was sort of hard to believe or remember that they were a link in long, sturdy chain that snaked out behind them. We've finally got out of the vestibule and into the crazy mansion of the internet where, if you haven't done anything recently, you may as well not have done anything at all. But even if Jim Guthrie had slipped your mind by 2005, you couldn't help but find something familiar about a peppy jingle that even people without TVs were starting to hear everywhere, a ditty that was becoming as ubiquitous in Canada as those kids banging anthemically on their safety gear.

In 2005, director Yael Staav had used Jim's song "Trust" from *A Thousand Songs* and an unreleased track, "Hug Me 'Til I'm Blue," in a series of award-winning commercials for the ALS[37] Society of Canada. "[The music] really did stand out at the time," says Ted Rosnick, of RMW Music, a 25-year-old audio production house in Toronto. "And I was very curious who this Jim Guthrie fellow was. At the time, in advertising, it was just on the cusp of the singer-songwriter thing. Much simpler, more intimate—Feist was just coming on—and Jim was one of those guys."

RMW was asked to do the music for a new Capital One campaign directed by The Perlorian Brothers. "Brilliant filmmakers[38]," explains Jim. "They've done some pretty fucked up ads. They're the kind of guys who grew up knowing that ads are a façade, knowing that nothing looks that good, or is as good [as it appears in the ad], and they've always seemed to use that disdain for that sort of 'corporate manipulation' as inspiration for their amazingly tweaked take on what an ad can be."

The Bros recommended Jim for the ad, so Ted brought him in and set him to work on the campaign.

"In some ways I had no business doing ad music," Jim admits, "but my naivety gave me an edge. I saw it as a challenge."

With no more direction than "sing what you see," Jim cranked out a couple of tries, all of which were passed on. "That was the first time I was making music to essentially please someone other than myself," says Jim, "and the rejection was rough. Since they were letting me do anything

---

37 Amyotrophic lateral sclerosis, aka Lou Gehrig's Disease.

38 A pseudonym "derived from the world 'perlorian' from the Greek word for monster (pelor). In botany it's used to describe the abnormal production of actinomorphic flowers in a plant of a species that usually produces zygomorphic flowers—in other words, a literal freak of nature. In Japanese slang it's used to refer to conformity—don't be normal."

I wanted, I was trying to be playful, trying to embrace the Ween inside of me. I was making an effort, I was owning it, and the rejection was so immediate.

"In a sort of desperation, in a feeling of 'fuck this process,' I sang the most non-melodic melody I could think of. 'Hands in my pocket, hands in my pocket, hands in my pocket.' To me, it was a total toss off. It was me taking the piss out of myself."

But the company loved Jim's piss-take, as did the focus groups.

"The great thing about Jim's music," says Ted, "why it sounds the way it sounds, is because Jim plays all the instruments, which I didn't know. There were a lot of flaws in the recording, but when you put it all together, it sounded great. It had this honest feeling to it. And I think that's why everyone gravitated to it so quickly."

Airing in the fall of 2005, the ad was quickly snapped up by popular culture here in Canada, from YouTube parodies, to political cartoons, to a full-on Yankovic-ing on the *Rick Mercer Report* about a year later. It wasn't long before "Jim Guthrie" became a requested style of music in the Toronto ad world.

"There was nothing else in Canada that sounded like I did," says Jim. "It wasn't because I'm a visionary or I know any better. It's just because I did what I did, and it worked. It was just the right time for it. It's what I'd been doing my whole life. It's *A Thousand Songs* to me. It's what's on [the Sonic Bunny] tapes. There's really no difference, except that now it's worth something to someone. I can get hired over and over again, and I'm not doing anything differently. Ad music seemed like honest work because after I had proved myself they were asking me to 'do what I do' and make my broken version of traditional ad music.

"When the 'Hands in My Pocket' thing took off, I at least finally felt accepted outside of my own community. I've never done a lot of touring as 'Jim Guthrie,' so I've struggled with that feeling of really breaking out of Guelph or Toronto."

Over a year, the shock of hearing Jim Guthrie in commercials turned into the confusion of whether or not that *was* Jim on the TV or radio.

"All of a sudden every company had their own Jim Guthrie," says Ted. "Was it as good and as smart? Probably not. But I think the general public doesn't know the difference after a while anyway. It definitely did dilute [Jim's sound]. But Jim isn't a one trick pony, either. He wasn't only writing these silly songs for us. He was also writing very emotional pieces of music. All kinds. He's a very talented, versatile guy."

Maybe the best measurement of Jim's ad scope is to put that first hit, "Hands in My Pocket," up to his next one, 2005's "Bring on the Night," for Jackson Triggs winery. One sounds nothing like the other, the former bongo-full and quirky, the latter softly fingerpicked and soulful. And both contained grist enough in their early ad incarnations that Jim was able to mill out full songs, "Hands" showed up on Jim's website for a spell, and "Bring" landed on Jim's most recent album, *Takes Time*.

With Three Gut shut down and Jim in no rush to put out another pop album, ad work came along at a choice time. These projects satisfied a need to continue with a type of experiment he'd begun at 16, while at the same time getting him out of the pantry. "Everything before was more like sonic scrap collecting. I seriously have no master plan. If the spirit moved me, my next record would be, like, sweeping a floor. The sound of me sweeping a floor. I feel like some people can't figure me out. I've always been grateful for those people who are like, 'Whatever. It's just what Jim does.' A lot of the time, there's people who want more to hold onto. They need more similar-sounding things. I think that's why, for some people, *Now, More Than Ever* seemed like a 'breakthrough record.' It seemed cohesive from start to finish. But, really, it's another version of the experiment. My ad music felt like experimental pop music to me.

"There's a point in your life where—somewhere in your teens or your twenties—you decide who you're going to be, or who you think you are, or what you should do. Early on, I was like, 'I'm gonna be a musician. And that's it.' But I also sorta bought into the idea that I had to make records, sell them, tour the world, and that's how I make my living. I never aspired to sell a million records, but I definitely aspired to pay the bills. It wasn't until I stopped being who I thought I should be and started being who I needed to be, that I started to feel free.

"And it was a way to reinvent myself and subvert the expectations I felt to make a new record. It was liberating."

The only track from Jim's first tape, *Home Is Where The Rock Is* that makes it onto *A Thousand Songs* is the oddly muscular, wanking, and entirely strange "I Don't Wanna Be A Rockstar," opening with Jim smashing the heating pans in the McDonald's lobby. It's an odd declaration to make, if only because it sheds light on its opposite sentiment. Few musicians would have stones enough to outright admit wanting to be a rock star, especially now that integrity has become such a serious issue to people. But it's a troubling dichotomy, especially for an artist like Jim, who never had much interest in playing live, no matter the heft and ease of the pre-show shit: if you want to make music for a living, does that imply you need to perform music for a living?

Chances are the first shards of music you heard in your life were jingles and theme songs, maybe video game music. And now you can stand in a group of coevals from different backgrounds and argue whether Nickleback is as valid as Arcade Fire, or whether Celine Dion's music is worth any more than her equivalent meat would be priced at the butcher's, but I guarantee that if one person begins to hum the *Full House* theme or the Sugar Crisps jingle, everyone else will join in. But culturally we're still reluctant to talk about commercial music the same way we would our favourite bands.

What it boils down to is where you want separate an Artist from someone whose job it is to make art. Is a three-minute song selling the idea of true, romantic love inherently more worthwhile than a 30-second piece of music selling the idea of a new 2-in-1 shampoo and conditioner? Maybe the difference is you make money doing the one, and you try and break even with the other.

"The indie rock circuit is a grind," says Jim, "and it can burn you out and not make you want to play or even make music. Driving around for 23 hours to play one hour of music for no money is hard and counterproductive."

"The older I get," says Nick Thorburn, who brought Jim into his Islands project and collaborated with him on

Human Highway[39], "the more my ideas about 'selling out' have changed. I think it's a very adolescent notion. I'm not supported by a benefactor or King. I want to keep making music and create for a living and that means making some compromises. For years, I would turn down money for use in commercials but it's not feasible. There's an ethical way to make a living so I try to adhere to that. All the noise about 'selling out' often has to do with the worry that your peers or your fans will judge you. And I categorically refuse to be motivated artistically or commercially by what other people think about me. I'm hungry!"

"There's just such a double standard," Jim continues, "if you're not a successful band, and you end up doing ad work and score work, writing for a product. But if you *are* a successful band, you *are* the product and that comes with its own special set of compromises and pitfalls. Over the years I've tried to intellectualize the meaning of selling out, but fuck it. I think it's a dated term. It's between the hippies and the yuppies. It's something kids can afford to shout about from the comfort of their parents' basement. I only really struggled with doing ad music because I couldn't believe someone was finally paying me to do what I love. If I had started doing ad music and then bought a Segway and ceased to explore all other musical pursuits, that would have been depressing. Or unfortunate. Depressingly unfortunate. But ad music was just another existential pay cheque."

While jingles jingled Jim at an ideal time professionally,

---

39 Nick achieved a new level of exposure in 2014 with his score to the hit podcast *Serial*.

they also loosened a ruthless self-editing that had been constipating him since *Now, More Than Ever*, opening him up to new ways and reasons to make music.

A few years ago, an iTunes search for "Jim Guthrie" would lead you to, amongst Jim's primary work, *Canadian Idol* winner Eva Avila's second single "I Owe it All To You." Jim's credited along with three other writers. The day Avila was crowned our Idol, a songwriting camp was held by Sony/ BMG. A horde of musicians were brought together to crank out pop for the singer. Anyone in a room that produces a song gets a songwriting credit. Thanks to Jim's increasing willingness to explore new ways of making music, he became a jewel in that Idol's crown.

"There was a time where saying yes to writing songs for a major label would've been totally against what I [stood] for. But I've learned that so many more good things can come from [saying] yes. When you're young, you say no to so much. You obviously don't want to lose yourself in 'yes,' but in this case the opportunity came up to work with musicians from all over the place. People who write songs for a living. People who write 300 songs per year that may never be heard by anybody. I was knocking heads with guys who had written songs for Celine Dion, Shania Twain, the Nylons, New Kids on the Block, Justin Bieber, and Anne Murray. I met dudes from Nashville. Super heavy-duty musicians who've written more songs than I've taken shits in my life.

"You should always be making and doing, because the alternative is to not to. And that's the greater crime. Not doing anything at all is so much worse than doing something that's shitty. I've been my own worst critic, my own worst editor, to the point where I'm editing so hard nothing's coming out. After all these years, those are my biggest regrets. Those times where I couldn't get out of my own way. You're allowed to make bad art. And even what you think's bad at the time may not be. It's just important that you do and then let time decide how good it is."

Though pretty firmly settled into the "I Don't Wanna Be A Rock Star" declaration he made at 18—and afforded it by his recent commercial success—Jim made a couple final sallies, both with Nick Thorburn.

"I'll never forget the first time I hard *Now, More Than Ever*," says Nick. "I was floored. Jamie [Thompson], the Unicorns drummer, grew up in Guelph and knew Jimmy and actually played on that record. We were driving from Montreal to Toronto to play a very early Unicorns show and we must've listened to that record the whole way. I was in awe. Both of our records[40] came out within a few weeks of each other, I believe. I'd heard and really liked Jim's stuff before this, but this vaulted him into a very esteemed place in my heart. That record continues to reveal new things about itself to me. Jim's songs have this uncanny ability to connect with me on such an intimate level, as though I'm the only listener he'd ever intended on having—as though these songs were being written as specific epistles directed squarely at me."

The Unicorns died in 2004, sort of phoenixing three years later as Islands, a project helmed by Nick and Jamie. "We

---

40 Nick's, with the Unicorns, was the internationally beloved corker, *Who Will Cut Our Hair When We're Gone?*

wanted Jim in the band," says Nick. "We were making the record and we had him come in and play guitar on 'Swans.' He actually only plays on the song's coda, but it's a memorable part. And he really embellished the Neil Young vibe I was aiming for. Jamie and I had convinced Jim to come out on the road, and it's amazing how long we got him for. He was in the band as long as Jamie for Christ's sake!"

Clad in white along with the rest of the band, Jim toured with Islands between September 2005 and May 2006.

"I don't think he was very happy to be away from his girlfriend (now wife) for such a long period of time," says Nick, "but we had some really good times. I'll never forget playing at SXSW at some awful backyard shithole with other bands' shitty music bleeding into our set, and I had taken some ecstasy and was so high I could barely stand up. I was trying to take off all my clothes. But I was in this pocket and I remember playing alongside Jim and we were just in this groove. I looked over at him and we just shared this look. And then he mouthed the words 'You're on fire!' It was quite the moment."

It was on the third leg of the Islands tour, in Tucson, Arizona, that the collaboration between Nick and Jim that would become the album *Moody Motorcycle*, started to get its tank filled. "I knew Jim's time was almost up with Islands, but I wanted to keep playing with him. I was strumming a song idly on the tour bus (those were days) and he pulled out a 4-track and we went up into the hotel room (Hotel Congress) and recorded the guitar and my vocals and then his harmony. We did it so fast and then I think we both knew we should make a whole record together. A year elapsed, but

I went up to Toronto in the summer of 2007 and we knocked it out in his bedroom in a week and half."

Under the name Human Highway, Jim and Nick released the album with Suicide Squeeze in August 2008. Evoking the harmonizing two-handers of the Everly Brothers, *Moody Motorcycle* feels effortless, like a laid-back pop conversation between two dudes who have honed their craft. Criticism of the album suggested that the songs were maybe too effortless, too laid-back from two musicians who were theretofore renowned for creating unique tension in staid pop formulas, but who cares. The album is quirky snapshot of Jim and Nick's relationship, made possible by the pressure taken off Jim thanks to his success with the ad work.

A month of mostly U.S. Human Highway shows in March 2009, would be Jim's final real tour to date. Living in Montreal at the time, Evan Clarke met up with Jim on the first date of Human Highway's tour. "I was like, 'How are ya, Jim?' And he was immediately, 'I just wanna be home.'"

"My biggest aspiration," says Jim, "was to own a house and fill the basement with noise makers. I have that now. I feel like I'm living out the other side of my musical fantasy, and that's to do exactly what I'm doing in film and TV, and most recently games. I've been so lucky."

It seems unfair to lay a life all out while it's still in progress. It's likewise bastardly to be far back enough to see how much Jim's success has had to do with being at the right place, at the right time, with the right people.

In talking with Jim's friends and collaborators, the subject of Jim's luck came up with nearly everybody. From Jim being lucky to not die in that rollover, to Jim being lucky that his name got dropped to the head of a music production company that had just been contracted to score Capital One's new campaign, Jim's been able to jump on a lot of trains as they smoke by. But let Aaron Riches remind you: "The most beautiful things in life are given accidentally."

It's fair to say that Jim's been lucky, but it would be a disservice to imply that Jim has just passively floated into good fortune. Artistically and professionally, it takes a special kind of chutzpa to have a life and process that's open to the possibility of both the best and the worst things happening. I think it's this that's so essentially good and honest about Jim's music. The stuff is full of a curiosity and an openness that, at the beginning of his songwriting and recording, he was able to reflect on tape, and later, as his chops got more meaty, that he was able to preserve.

"Every song was an accident," Jim says of his work, "Every song was a gift. I never saw myself as knowledgeable, as able to repeat a moment. Everything's kinda fleeting. You can always copy yourself, but does it lead to that special place that gives art meaning, and your reason to do it meaning? Every song I'd started started with the assumption that I didn't know what I was doing. I know what the feeling's like, and I've honed my craft enough that I know how to wrestle it to the ground and hogtie it. I can better capitalize on the little moments."

After the idea of luck has been brought up with Jim's friends, along comes the thought game of "What if Jim hadn't been lucky?" The answer is the same across the board: Jim would still be making music, just not getting paid for it. Other than the paycheque, very little would be different.

"I don't know anybody who deserves the success they've had as much as Jim," says Stephen Evans. "In a way, it's so brave of him. It is a kind of gamble to not go to school after high school, and just put yourself into music and work shitty jobs to get by."

When I put the "What if…" question to Stephen, he gets around to the same conclusion as everyone else, but his initial reaction skirts towards a more intimate honesty.

"What if Jim hadn't been so lucky?"

"God," he says. "What an awful thought."

CHAPTER 6

An Experimental Cure for Acute Soul-Sickness

"The mysterious musical fellow known as Jim Guthrie
said he was ready to play a little song if we wanted to give
it a listen. Jim invited us to take a seat by the fire."
– *Superbrothers: Sword & Sworcery* EP

Craig D. Adams, the hub of Superbrothers, moved to Toronto in the early 2000s to attend Sheridan College—the same school Jim might have studied at had he not purposely bungled his hand study. "Somebody must've given me a copy of *Alone at the Microphone* at the time," Craig remembers. "I guess I just kinda like whatever [Royal City] is: very sort of honest, naked, poetic, and small and beautiful. I didn't know anything about Jim Guthrie, though."

Perusing a record store adjacent to Three Gut HQ, Craig found *Morning Noon Night* in the Recommended display. "[The blurb] must have said something about how Jim was using a PlayStation. So I was like, 'Oh, weird. One of the rock stars from Royal City is clearly a nerd.'

"I loved the hell out of *Morning Noon Night*. I listened to it about a million times," he says. "And then *Now, More Than Ever* came out, and I had another Jim album to chew on. Around that time, I was out of art school, and those albums were on heavy rotation. If I was working on a project late at night it would be Caribou, I am Robot [and Proud], a whole whack of Jim Guthrie."

Out of school and looking for design jobs, Craig started to disseminate samples of his work to art directors. "But I knew that [most people] would have little interest in [my] work," he says of his pixelated aesthetic. "It was too early, before the indie game phenomena. My kind of stupid plan was to figure out who would like it, and then send it to them. Jim Guthrie was on that list. This lo-fi, pixel style, to me, is in the exact same key as a lot of Jim's work—but specifically the kind of PlayStation-y, toy computer stuff on *Morning Noon Night*. I just had a feeling that if he's able to produce this music, he would probably enjoy whatever [the pixel art] is on some level."

In explaining 8-bit pixel art, Superbrothers casts a long, wide net: "Using individual blocks of colour to form a precise visual statement is a technique that dates back through the ages at least as far as 4th-century Macedonia," they write on their website, "arguably reaching its apex with the Christian mosaics of the Byzantine empire eight centuries later."

Those of us not so hip to visual archaeology are probably familiar with these "grid-based" images[41] from early video games—those "electronic amusements of yesteryear," in

---

41 A pixel being "that most basic unit of electronic display."

Superbrothers' parlance. It's a suggestive aesthetic, where a more detailed image is implied by a careful arrangement of rudimentary components. On a design level, the lo-fi visual style falls in line with the essentials of image making described by Scott McCloud in *Understanding Comics*. "Amplification through simplification," McCloud terms it. "By stripping down an image to its essential 'meaning,'" he writes, "an artist can amplify that meaning in a way that that realistic art can't."

The more simplified, the easier it is for the audience to find themselves in the piece.

Jim responded to Craig's mailer with a disc of 10 unreleased songs, "an instrumental record that's like the score for some weird movie that doesn't exist." These were the PlayStation kin of those glitchy volleys on *Morning Noon Night*[42].

"Apparently this is a pattern," says Craig, who wouldn't hear about Jim's Royal City Home Rock Eruption until years later. "Fledgling artists or musicians send Jim something and if he thinks it's cool, if it resonates with him, he'll pick up the phone, or put it on a radio show."

Craig had been flirting with game making, but couldn't get his means and his ambition to gel. "I had committed to going in this direction for whatever reason," he says, "and it was kind of a dead end. I didn't have the mental power to dig myself out of these ditches I was getting into. I was changing gears when Jim's disc showed up."

The changed gears became films with a video game feel, set to Jim's tracks "Children of the Clone" and "Dot Matrix Revolution." Like Jim's sensibility, the animation is a chat

---

42 Released as *Children of the Clone* in December 2011.

between playfulness and earnestness. A bit washed out, almost over-exposed, the quality of the image imbues the seemingly inorganic pixel style and character movement with lifelike quality. Like the track itself, a digitizing and mangling of an analogue sound, Craig's animation makes the unreal real-feeling. "I was trying to provide a window into the tune," Craig demurs, "so you could see what's already happening in the song. I'm just a Jim Guthrie delivery service."

If you had gainful interest in video games in the mid-2000s, you went to Vancouver, home of the likes of Capcom, or Montreal, which boats Ubisoft and EA. Industry-wise, Toronto boasted jack. Shaw-Han Liem, AKA I am Robot and Proud and co-designer of *Sound Shapes*[43], recalls that time: "There were a bunch of young people in Toronto," he says, "that were all basically graduating from [design and technology] programs, interested in making games, but there was no one hiring them. They all just started doing their own thing, making their own games. If Ubisoft had been in Toronto, all these 25-year-olds would've just got jobs there. And probably none of this would've happened."

That "this" is a surge of DIY game making. Better, more affordable technologies made design easier, and innovations in how games were bought and played kicked down the door for distribution. "In 2005, things were definitely changing," says Craig. Mare and Raigan's game *N*, in terms of origin and destination, was one of the first major steps towards indie

---

43 An interactive music-making game featuring contributions from the likes of Beck, Deadmou5, and Jim, as well as art from Superbros.

gaming. "Xbox 360 had a download service, so you could buy a cheap, small game. That was a major limiting factor. If you're a little person, making a little expressive thing, you're not going to print it on a disc, put it in a box, and try and sell it in a store. This new functionality definitely opened the door. *N* was made with passion. But it also found this big, enthusiastic audience. Then, on the expressive and musical side, was John Mak[44]'s *Everyday Shooter* on the PS3. He made it entirely on his own. Every level [of the game] is a song that John made. I was a super big fan. And I probably heard that he was in Toronto sharing the same air space. That was pretty inspiring."

As mainstream games were moving towards more expansive, limitless worlds, the crews building them had to likewise become enormous, creating a generation of games that, while rich in detail, were soft in personality. The same way that punk, and, later, indie rock, was a recalibration of why, how, and by whom music gets made, indie games balked the trend, favouring smaller creative crews and larger personality.

"Maybe one of the reasons I was attracted to the Three Gut stuff was that's the way I thought stuff should be done," Craig reflects. "You make a thing you believe in, and hopefully your friends are on a similar wavelength, and that creates a scene."

In 2003, the development studio Capybara Games began out of frustration with the lack of organized opportunities for game developers in Toronto. They hit their stride with 2008's puzzle game *Critter Crunch*. Aware of Craig's pixel art, the two parties bumped into each other and struck up a deal. Craig pitched the idea of involving his "nerd" buddy Jim Guthrie.

---

44 Co-creator of *Sound Shapes*.

When Jim was looped in the project, there was talk about the name, the aesthetic, *The Legend of Zelda* and *Castlevania* were brought up as reference points. Jim kicked in some suitable songs, and Craig and his team began to let those shape the art and story, which then started to shape Jim's compositions. *Sword & Sworcery* is another one of those super soups of influence. Jim's initial PlayStation started the ball rolling, and from there, Craig, creative director Kris Piotrowski and Jim would toss ideas into the pot, assisted by Jon Maur and Frankie Leung, who, Jim says, "stitched it all together with 1s and 0s."

Superbrothers: Sword & Sworcery EP takes its first move from the playbook of a tipsy chubber who's sweet on you: it puts headphones on you, insisting, "You need to hear this."

We're beamed onto a platform in a sylvan clearing with fireflies or motes of magic drifting around us. Insects trill, frogs crank, and there's the barely perceptible sound of wind on water. The only instructions we're given are, "Look. Touch. Listen." Only after we meet a woodsman named Logfella do we find out that we're—whoever we are—on an errand, a "woeful" one at that. When Jim's "Lone Star" kicks in—with a digitized-sounding stand-up bass and a jittering, clapping beat reminiscent of the opening of *Morning Noon Night*—we get the idea that whatever it is we're doing is important and epic.

In a visual essay that preceded *Superbrothers: Sword & Sworcery EP*, "Less Talk More Rock," Superbrothers spoke out against the prevalence of instruction in narrative games: "Remember when Miyamoto[45] made that video

---

45 Shigeru Miyamoto, creator of Donky Kong, Mario, and Zelda.

game about those plumbers?" they write. "The real revolution with that video game was in the style of communication... Coins looked like they sounded and they sounded the way they behaved in the context of the mechanics.

"It didn't need to talk much at all," Superbrothers goes on, "it was pure rock. This was the native language of video games: synesthetic audiovisual expressing a meaning, where sound and image and logic come together and feel right, where the communication is nonverbal but nonetheless articulate."

Superbrothers: Sword & Sworcery EP inevitably gives in to talk over rock in order to drip details into our character's identity and the nature of our woeful errand—finding a Megatome, batting some Trigons, making it on time for a rock show. But this talk is sparse. The game doesn't hold your hand. It will lay out some explanation, but for the most part you're on your own in this lush, pixelated world.

"I got to the first boss battle, where you fight the first trigon," says Adam Hammond, who taught the game in a university course covering digital-only literature. "And I remember it was a breakthrough for me to beat this thing. My heart was beating fast—I'm not good at video games, I'm not gonna know how to do this—but it was a matter of chilling out and letting the music tell you what to do."

Not really giving a piss in the pool about solving puzzles or beating level bosses myself, it was the walking that stood out to me—a frustrating demand if you're eager to burn through the game. This is not an errand that rewards impatience, requiring you to cross and re-cross screens to fetch an item or information, only to find you've got to go back to where you set out from. You're forced to live in this world, immersed in

97

the soundscape and art of it. Playing it again, in the context of writing this section, the first thing I thought of was the sound of walking that opens *Victim of Lo-fi*, the sound of insect babble and the throat clearing of distant thunder bringing to mind the phone interruption in "Roads and Paper Routes."

"The game really wants you to not rush through[46]," says Adam, "and I think the music creates a more contemplative space, it slows you down. You only progress in the game if you stop trying obsessively to figure it out, if you take it easy and listen to the music. It's not just there to entertain you; it's a part of the story. The game seems to want, more than anything else, to create a mood in the mind of the player."

If the game is a happy marriage of Craig and Jim's creative sensibilities it's likewise a representation of their sensibilities of creating. As The Scythian—a female warrior in a new land—we move forward with little awareness of where we're headed, propelled by the desire to test and discover, as opposed to some teleological drive to complete. We turn up the amps and go. By being stingy with instructions and narrative, the game can't help but become a simulation of a creative, collaborative experience. You learn the game, the same way you struggle through figuring out the guitar, say, or moonwalking. To play through, you need to make peace with failure, get comfortable with the art of fucking up.

Superbrothers: Sword & Sworcery EP was launched in March 2011. Jim's expanded soundtrack, *Sword & Sworcery*

---

46 The game is specifically married to the lunar cycles, and depending on what the moon's up to outside your window, you may have to wait until the satellite enters a new phase to continue.

LP: The Ballad of the Space Babies, followed in April. A thousand copy run of vinyl, done as a bit of lark, sold out lickety-split. Since it's release, it's sold more copies than all of Jim's other releases combined.

"*Sword & Sworcery* received universal acclaim," says Rich Vreeland, AKA Disasterpeace, much-lauded composer for the game *FEZ*, "and Jim's equal billing is well deserved, as the music is a massive part of the experience. Jim really did something fresh for [that game], in bringing the maturity of his musical career to the sphere of games. A lot of the music in games is self-referential, playing on tropes and clichés that have been established in game culture over the last 30 to 40 years. Jim's work on *Sworcery* was an excellent example of ignoring most of that and doing something completely different, and quite successfully."

Jim had already done stalwart score work for the documentaries *The Bodybuilder and I* and *When We Were Boys*, but it was his *Sword & Sworcery* work that caught the ears of documentarians Lisa Pajot and James Swirksy. At the time they were halfway through a project that would become a gateway and introduction to this new DIY movement in games: *Indie Game: The Movie*.

"We were about halfway done editing [when] we started emailing with Jim," says James. "*Sword & Sworcery* had come out midway through our shoot. We loved it. It was so inspiring and frustrating at the same time; something so good that you wish you made it. And the music was a huge part of that. We thought Jim would be a no go. We figured he was too big. But when we got home we shot him an email."

"And he responded in, like, an hour," laughs Lisanne. "We showed him a two-hour rough cut. His response was amazing, full of expletives. 'It's fucking amazing.' He was the very first person to see anything.

"He's such a good composer," Lisanne continues. "I don't know how he thinks backwards, but Jim can find moments, emotional moments, and make his melodies work to hit those beats. We didn't realize this ahead of time, how Jim's talent of understanding the emotional backbone of a scene, is incredibly useful in scoring. The music rode the background and foreground perfectly. That wasn't obvious to me until I listened to the standalone album."

As he did with *Sword & Sworcery*, Jim released a fleshed-out soundtrack for *Indie Game*, and both those albums have gone on to enjoy a hearty second life. "Jim is the background for so many creative people," says Lisanne. "Especially with coding and graphic arts. There's no singing, so it makes it easier to open. I think he was surprised, when he put out these albums, that there was so much support. And I think why those albums have done so well is people see value in them being a part of their process."

"Lots of visual-based artists have messaged me telling me [those] soundtracks really lube the tubes for them," Jim confirms.

"[Jim's] music is not forcing a pace for the work," says Felipe Budinich, a Chile-based game developer. "Instead, you get a very subtle undercurrent, an atmosphere. Jim's work simmers in the background, subtly influencing us. Like the sun entering the room through the window. It's not blinding you, but you know it's there, and it feels good."

In the indie rock community, Jim's soundtrack success has been mostly treated anecdotally, some interesting things that he did to make money between "real" albums. A lot of *Now, More Than Ever* and Royal City fans know about "Jim's video game stuff" and think it's neat, but don't hold it in the same esteem as that "non-video game" work.

When the opportunity to do a book about Jim presented itself around 2012, I was likewise dumb to Jim's newfound success, of this huge audience that had discovered and employed his work. Passing through Toronto on a book tour that spring, I met with Jim to pitch the idea of this book. I gifted him the story collection I had just released, and he passed off a *Sword & Sworcery* vinyl. Still, I thought of the game stuff more as a neat little aside.

That summer I was in Arizona working on some other project, and I finally got around to putting on the album. I had it on in my rental car and kept it on repeat while I puttered through those sere, empty landscapes. Jim had described the music to me as "an epic loneliness," and that about defined that road trip. I hadn't really adopted music like that since walking through Montreal listening to *A Thousand Songs* in my headphones a decade earlier.

"Sometimes I feel like the Three Gut days were a lifetime ago," says Jim, "and I'm starting all over again with indie games.

"I find instrumental more freeing these days, so there's been that struggle cause I know some people would rather I sing them a song than do soundtracks[47]. I'd much rather

---

47 In 2013, Jim scored *The Manor*, a documentary about Guelph's venerable strip club.

influence people in subtle ways versus having the hit of the summer. This is the kind of thing I'm a little obsessed with. This kind of subtly ominous influence on the masses. Not exactly Muzak, but something like it. In some ways I'd love to be the shoehorn or coat hanger of music. An omnipresent influence that effects people everyday but little thought goes into where it came from or who's behind it.

"I guess my ad [and] my film work fulfilled some of those fantasies. It's a tricky thing to make music that's felt but not heard. In film I'm trying not to distract from the scene and knock the viewer out of the moment. Sometimes music is most effective when it's as subconscious as the wrinkles on the actors face."

For a guy with no interest in being the centre of attention, Jim found the perfect compromise—or, the perfect compromise found him. He found a way to be the centre of something inside you, the listener, to the point where you're not sure if how you're responding and feeling is him, or if it's you, or if it's a mix of both.

"I was thinking about my yin yang with being the frontman of a band vs. sideman," he says, "and writing pop songs vs. background, supporting score music and how I've tired to balance the two, but I'm mostly siding with being in the background. Having said that, I'm still a little blown away that I'll be the subject of a book. If I get a book, then everyone else should get a book, too.

"Is there anyway you can write me in as a supporting character in my own biography?"

Jim finally released *Takes Time*, ostensibly the follow-up to

Now, More Than Ever, in May 2013. He had begun in 2007, recording with Mark Lawson[48] at the Arcade Fire church in Farnham, QC. Jim brought Simon Osborne and Evan Clarke along. "We went into that recording unprepared," says Evan. "It was one of those things where you scheduled a date and assumed you'd be ready by then." In the six years between the sessions and the release, Jim tinkered with and reimagined those initial bed tracks into an album that manages to harmoniously represent all of Jim's seemingly disparate musical interests.

Most of the press and the reviews for *Takes Time,* maybe to remind readers who this guy was, introduced Jim as "influential," but didn't go much further than that.

Influence-wise, Jim's friends make for a good opening paragraph: he had Arcade Fire open for him, was involved in a label that gave a jump to the sapped battery of Canadian music, and *Now, More Than Ever* was a showcase for Owen Pallett's prowess. But what does any of that mean?

I get that part of my "woeful errand" in writing this book is articulating that influence, establishing why you should care about Jim Guthrie, if you don't already.

"I don't know if his influence could ever be fully gauged," says Michael Barclay. "I don't hear a lot of bands that sound like Jim Guthrie. But if you look at all the people that he's... he does sort of have a Midas touch about him. People like Owen, The Constantines, Arcade Fire, Feist... They were all drawn to him. They obviously don't sound like Jim, but

---

48 Mark's fiddled the board knobs for the likes of Arcade Fire, The Unicorns, Isalnds, Owen Pallett, Timber Timbre, Beirut

at early, crucial points in their careers, they found him inspiring. His music seems effortless, like it flows out of him naturally. Maybe that's something those artists envy, if they have a laborious writing process, Jim makes it seem so easy."

"I think a lot of people try to compartmentalize their life," offers Mike Olsen, "try and prepare for what's coming next. And I think Jim's someone with a healthy spirit, a healthy idea of the fact that he has no fucking clue about what's coming next in his life. Hence: he's a gambler. Hence: he's a chance taker. He's, 'Fuck it. Yeah, I'll do that.' He's really inspiring. It's part of the character. It's part of what makes you an artist and a musician. You take a chance, because life already is that anyway. You're just admitting it."

Jim's influence is essentially creative, I'd hazard. The guy and his work are a breathing permission to do your own thing, carrying on the creative permission given to him by people like Steve McCuen and Gord High and Aaron Riches. Whether you're Feist or some kid screwing around on GarageBand, there's something about what Jim does, what his music exudes, that makes you want to do something for yourself.

"We played basketball this one time," remembers Colin Clark, "and Jim could hit a massive three pointer backwards with his eyes closed. The whole works. He can just do stuff that, for us, is unbelievable."

And what happens when you see a guy easily sinking trick threes? Your first impulse it to try it yourself, before considering the kind of work and time it takes to make anything look easy and fun.

"Jim doesn't have a work ethic," explains Aaron Riches. "I mean, he gets up at five o'clock in the morning and starts working, but he doesn't punch the clock. In my eyes, Jim has never worked a day in his life. He's done some things when he's needed to, like go set up chairs at some banquet. I think of Jim as a wonderfully free person."

"Jim really treated music like an art form early on," says Tim Kingsbury. "When I started out, I was trying to emulate everything, you know, buying guitar magazines. With Jim, he was creating these sound collage-y, arty little pop pieces. Very original. For me that was really influential. He admitted early on just how much sound and music meant to him and he explored it wholeheartedly. Jimmy has kind of stayed the same. He hasn't had a personality change or a shift in goals, or a shift in direction. It seems like what he was working towards just really grew around him. I find him really inspiring in that way, too."

"I think it was because of that disposition that made me realize what I'm good at," says Jim, "and sent me on a journey that I never would have been on. It's not even that wild a story, but personally... I think it's a pretty neat place to be, considering who I thought I was, or how shitty I thought things were, or how stricken with fear I was, or how hard I thought it would be. Like, I had no idea what I was gonna do up until I found music. Music basically gave me the courage to do a lot of things. In all my songs, on all my tapes, I would always sing about it: just a sound leading you somewhere."

The work that Jim did in 2014 is not that much different than 1994. The acumen has maybe changed, but the curiosity and warmth has stayed uncorrupted. Of course, who hears what he does has grown and changed, but his own interest and the pursuit hasn't budged much. That interest in learning new ways to explore what he can do with sound, or what sound can do with him. That there are albums, that Jim's issued something that makes it all the way to us for us to include in our own lives, feels like a happy accident of his consistent willingness to explore.

"I love how he just gets to keep playing," says Beate. "I feel like he still delights in everything he does. He still has that same great, adventurous spirit. Nothing that he's done has taken any of that essence away form him. So I think of him being the same person, even though I know that he's changed. *Grown-up* is not the right term; he's just has a better self-understanding."

"And he's apparently got the same haircut," I add.

"Pretty much," Beate laughs. "And he dresses the same, too."